Bawdy Baby-Boomer Bar-Room Bard!

Bawdy Baby-Boomer Bar-Room Bard!

Eric W. Fotherby

DESIGNED AND EDITED BY KATHY MIERZWA

ERIC FOTHERBY ENTERPRISES

Published in the United States of America

Library of Congress Control Number:
2017911702

ISBN: 978-0-9986259-1-1

Cover design by Kathy Mierzwa

FIRST EDITION
Printed in the United States of America
10 9 8 7 6 5 4 3 2 1

DEDICATION

For Mrs. Marilyn Prell,
my Creative Writing Teacher
at Mott High School
in Warren, Michigan in 1968.

She taught a shy, teenage boy
with low self-esteem (and no writing ability)
how to write creatively and appreciate the fine arts,
while giving him inner pride and self respect.

I am forever grateful.

I hope these literary selections of mine
will find a published form,
and an appreciative audience.
And that the final result
will meet with her much-desired approval!

Eric

EDITOR'S NOTES

How I came to be working on this book with Eric is an amazing story in itself. We first met in high school in Mrs. Prell's creative writing class in1968. I was the perky girl with the short-short Sassoon haircut and he was tall, skinny, and blond with an 'aw, shucks' laugh that made me want to laugh along with him.

We both were good writers, and two of Prell's Pets. After graduation Eric left Michigan and headed for Alaska; and after two years of college, I left the state on my bicycle, pedaling to Boston, where I've been ever since.

In March of 2001 my husband and I were sitting in the Boston Design Center chatting with our interior designer, waiting for rush-hour traffic to die down. I casually asked Marta where she was from, and she said "a suburb of Detroit that you've never heard of - Warren, Michigan."

I promptly exclaimed "I'm from Warren Michigan!" and we quickly established that we both had lived on the same street, three miles apart from each other, during the same time period in the 1960s. What an amazing coincidence!

Now Marta lived in a tiny town in New Hampshire, a very long way from Detroit. Interestingly, a woman in her town's garden club had taught in my Warren high school at some point - she asked did I know a Marilyn Prell?

I was incredulous! "Mrs. Prell! She was my favorite high school teacher. I became a writer and editor, thanks to her!" Somehow Mrs. Prell had left Michigan too, and was now living just 50 minutes away from me! What a small world after all!

Marilyn and I reunited right away, awed at our journeys; we have become good friends, seeing and calling each other regularly ever since then.

Fast forward to 2009, when Marilyn was retiring after teaching English, Writing and Literature for 44 years. I was invited to her retirement party, and thought it would be pretty cool if I could track down some of her former students from my class to see if they had continued writing, and would put together a tribute for Mrs. Prell.

I found Eric Fotherby by googling his unusual name (there are only two Eric Fotherbys in the world; the other is in England), searching online for his phone number and then cold-calling him. Indeed he had started writing again, and said he would love to contact Mrs. Prell and let her know how influential she had been to him.

When they talked on the phone she asked him that all-important author's question—"Have you been published yet?" Eric hadn't, but that set his wheels in motion to start writing in earnest and then to try to find a publisher.

Last year he called and asked if I had a literary agent or knew of how he could find one. I didn't, but we talked about writing and I gave him some encouragement for his publishing venture.

Eric diligently wrote letters to over 140 agents; he had the creative idea to pen his letter in the form of a rhyming poem ("Letter of Intent" on page 3). Alas, those potential agents weren't interested, so when that didn't work out, Eric continued his quest to be immortalized in print by finding an online publishing house who would take on the task of printing and marketing his book (even though they hadn't published any poetry before).

I heard from Eric again after said publishing house did a first edit on his poems; they had red-lined and ravaged his work. Perfectly-chosen words were eliminated, incorrect punctuation was inserted, rhymes were ruined and cadences changed. Eric told me that it was like his poems were edited by someone who didn't understand English! And worse, they wouldn't even let him speak to his editor—at all! That was totally unacceptable.

Eric asked if would I edit his poems, as I was likely to be a better editor than his publisher's people. I wasn't into poetry, didn't read poetry, and had never edited poetry, where the rules of grammar, punctuation and sentence structure go out the window.

"It'll only take a couple of days," he pleadingly promised.

Well, nine months and over 1000 exchanged e-mails later, his poems are ready for prime time. His poems were in good shape when I started, and at first I didn't think his voice needed editing at all. But after enjoyably reading his witty words over and over, I saw that there were details that needed clarifying, punctuation that required consistency and intriguing stories that warranted embellishing.

Eric ditched his so-called publishing company when we discovered it was a foreign scam (with hundreds of other dissatisfied authors!) and I worked out a book design and cover for him so we could self-publish the book exactly the way he wants it.

We've worked hard and had a fun time, while learning a lot. I learned how to improve his old snapshots in the always-intimidating Photoshop editing program and am so pleased with my new photo-transforming skills.

From him I learned about sonnets, sasquatches, the Seahawks, slander, spelling and Dr. Seuss. From me Eric learned about punctuation, publishing, photography, publicity, past participles and poetry slams.

I really like Eric's style and his humor. I've been impressed by his vast vocabulary (*Arabic Jinn? raiment?*) and his insistence that I not make him dumb down his words by suggesting more-commonly used descriptors. "Let my readers look them up in the dictionary!" he would exhort.

I've been impressed by the variety of topics that he writes about — from fruit flies to God, Napoleonic history to subterranean civilizations, the wreck of a cargo ship to his personal bowel-cleansing formula!

Most of all, I've never worked with anyone with such wholehearted willingness and devoted determination to keep rewriting and reworking to make their writing even better.

I've immensely enjoyed working with him on his dream project. Together we've achieved this rewarding result by doing what we both do best—writing—as taught and encouraged by our beloved Mrs. Marilyn Prell.

Kathy Mierzwa
April 2017

AUTHOR'S NOTES

Clinton Leroy Fotherby, my paternal Grandfather, was born in 1902 during the Klondike Gold Rush. Although he lived in Detroit, Michigan, he always held romantic aspirations of panning for gold in Alaska and the Yukon.

As a young boy of seven or eight, my Grandfather gave me two books to read and keep. One was "Songs of a Sourdough," and the other was "Ballads of a Cheechako." Both were written by Robert W. Service about the Alaska Gold Rush. This was my very first exposure to poetry, and these books were a personal and precious gift that I realized was my doorway to different worlds.

Service was a lauded poet, and known as "The Bard of the Yukon." His adventurous travels fueled his humorous, rhyming verses; I assumed that this was how great storytelling was done.

As a youth, I really did not write anything poetic, (except of the Roses-are-Red genre in Elementary School), until I signed up for a High School Creative Writing class, where I wrote a couple of poetic ditties to fulfill assignment requirements. I did not think they were very good, but was really very surprised when they turned out to be quite popular, and were published in the class writing book. Mrs. Prell was my teacher and mentor who planted the seed in my mind that I could actually be a Writer.

As a young student, reading books was the antidote to being housebound during long Michigan winters (and with only three TV channels to pick from at the time). I admired Faulkner and Hemingway, and I was very big on Michener and later on, Gary Jennings.

Although my grandfather never made it to Alaska, I made a beeline for the 49th state the day after I graduated High School. The poem, "West By Northwest to Alaska," is my story of that epic adventure from Michigan to Alaska, on page 239.

When the Seattle Seahawks football team went on their first Superbowl run in 2006 against the Steelers, it was very impelling and intoxicating for us to be on the national football radar. Later when the Seahawks were making their second Super Bowl run in 8 years in 2014, I got caught up in the enthusiasm and felt inspired to write motivational fan poetry about them and their lopsided (48-3) defeat of the Denver Broncos for their first Super Bowl victory in franchise history. That is when my poetry career was born. (It was perfect timing, now that I was retired and really didn't have much of anything important to do anyway).

I tested my poems on my sisters, who liked them, but they had no interest in football, and suggested that I branch out into some new subject matter. My friend Hans the Mailman, after hearing many of my tavern stories of travel experiences and adventures as a young man, suggested that I record them for posterity.

I took their advice and started to write in earnest in 2014. I was surprised at how easily the verses came spilling forth out of my brain, through my fingertips and into my computer. Sometimes I felt like I was being moved by the Holy Spirit, because I would awaken two hours earlier in the morning, sit down at the computer, and my fingers would fly as the words just flowed, bounced and danced lightly onto the screen. I liked to write long sentences and use eloquent, interesting words that I had found in the Thesaurus.

Of course I would rewrite and polish them many times, as a blacksmith sharpens his knife, and I could always find room for improvement. But after a year-and-a-half of that, I decided it was time to bring them out of my computer's Documents File, and attempt to get them published to share with the world.

I quickly found out that getting something published is much more difficult than the actual writing!

After failing to accomplish this on my own, I connected with a fellow former writing classmate who had continued writing after high school. Even though we hadn't seen each other in almost 50 years and we now live on opposite

coasts, we worked together diligently for several months to bring this book to fruition. Kathy would edit and make good suggestions, and I would dutifully rewrite and refine. When my book designer-agreement fell through, Kathy consented to design the whole manuscript as well. She worked with my old travel saga snapshots (learning Photoshop skills in the process) and selected all the images to embellish the stories. She chose fonts and spacings and created the perfect book cover. My never-ending appreciation of her skills and patience to complete this project will never be forgotten. Together we have created a much richer and much more substantial and enterprising book that we can both be immensely proud of.

I hope that my readers will find velvet in my verses and pleasure in my prose! This literary work has been my indulgence, my gratification and my contentment. I have strived to tell a story half as well as Robert Service; if I have accomplished that, at least then I will be able to shamelessly and humbly call myself an Author.

Eric W. Fotherby

April 2017

CONTENTS

SELF

FAMILY

LIFE

MISCELLANEOUS

OPINION

POETRY FORMS

POLITICS

SPORTS

SENIORITY

TRAVEL EPICS

Dram Shop Ditty

I drink my fill of foamy ale
I sing a song, I tell a tale,
        I play the fiddle;
My throat is chronically dry,
Yet savant of a sort am I,
        And Life's my riddle.

- Robert W. Service

Self

A LETTER OF INTENT

I have written some massive, maximal Epics,
In a royal preeminent poetic Book,
And I would be quite honored,
If you would take the time
For a critical, good look.
Scrutinize my rhymes
Indubitably hard.
I zestfully call it:
Bawdy Baby-Boomer Bar-Room Bard!

I have been most careful
For you not to squander your time,
While you joyfully peruse
What is most probably,
Entirely so remarkably,
Agelessly-sentimental,
Exceptionally-pleasing
Exquisitely-fine rhymes.

My goal is to be published,
So I am looking for an enlightened Agent,
Possibly one with just a little more patience,
To sacrifice some of their time for a look,
At my late-in-life, so recently-written,
But still-very-germane, poetry book.
Browsing through Agents' exclusive categories,
Remarkably, I found them lacking and wanting;
They did not aspire or have any desire

For superlatively-captivating poetic stories.
The glaring absence of poetry,
Omitted most inappropriately.
Quaint, unoffending affectations,
Unpretentious dissertations.
Emotional reminiscences,
Romantic, earthly worldliness.
My sometimes-clever allegories.
Truth telling, is not ever boring.

Many soulful, introspective insights,
Experiences shared freely from my life,
Mixing it in with a little personal strife.
Pieces and intriguing fragments,
Some provocative entertainment,
Captivating stimulation,
Engrossing fascination,
Enthralling relaxation!
Sometimes jumping, in leaps and bounds,
Towards unusual perceptions of reality.
I've found some of my stories may astound,
I will not waste your time with any banality.

A compendium of Seattle Seahawk dissertations,
Also, a few Mariner baseball designations.
From there I began to write,
About the human vagaries of life.

My sisters had urged and entreated me,
To please do discover different diversities.

Explore various externalized emotions:
Ecstasy, elation, and human commotion!
They said I needed to expand like an ocean,
That I should broaden and branch myself out,
Increase and amplify my artistic horizons;
They said they did not have any doubts!

A few Ballads and Sonnets,
Stimulating, and trendy, do tell,
Even a few classic Villanelles!
Yes, of course, some ribald Limericks,
Also a selection of Haikus and Quotes,
Lilting lightly, little ditties, poetic rotes.

I have descriptively illustrated,
With some personal pictures.
And some moderate mixtures,
Of irradiant illuminating pictures,
I have about 100 poems.
That most often range
Around two to eight pages or so.
One epic poem surges way overboard,
I counted at least 80 pages or more;
I guarantee that no one will get bored!

It is a most excellent, good book.
You would be most wise to consider,
To inquisitively open the cover,
And take a contemplative, long look.

So if you are intrigued by my boast,
In having your readers intensely engrossed,
In insightful, penetrating poems with some prose,
A place where one can deeply bury their nose.
Then it would best behoove all of you,
To seek some good fortune and pursue,
A contract for this elegantly-refined book,
That I devotedly have so lovingly produced.
So this grievously-lost art form,
Can be retroactively revived and renewed!

Now since I have become happily retired,
I have recently found the free time,
Waxing and whiling away hours sublime,
Narrating some of my favorite stories,
With a beat that's high-stepping in time,
Irrationally, incomprehensibly written in rhyme,
For true poetry devotees
Who appreciate tuned literary chimes.

My lofty goal is to be published,
So I can share them sometime!
Employing my passé literary style,
Celebrating my life, without any guile.
Revealing some unique and riveting drama
In a distinguished and memorable genre.

From you, it is your esteemed expertise
That is what I so very much need;
Introduce my work to a Publisher

Lacking credentials, still unimpeded,
So that a mesmerized audience,
Will most enthusiastically be entreated.

Maybe you can exploit me,
As live bait on your hook,
To ascertain a capable Firm,
Who just might take a good long look,
And desire to publish,
A most delightful, fantastic book!

BEING YOUNG

Being young, for me, was so much fun—
The center of attention, the Spoiled One.
At six weeks old, as soon as I was able,
While getting my dirty diapers changed,
I rolled right off of the kitchen table;
Landed on my head, my brain rearranged.

It may be why, compared to my siblings,
(And I don't want to appear to be quibbling),
But according to all of the public school charts,
I didn't end up quite as technically smart.

At nine months old I was able to run.
I have the photographic proof,
I was a little Son Of A Gun;
I was my Mother's First Born.
I was pampered and coddled,
In nice, clean white clothes;
I was cuddled and swaddled.
Adored and admired,
I was lovingly nuzzled and snuggled.

When my milk bottle was empty,
I did not dawdle at all,
I threw that breakable glass bottle.
I hurled it from my crib, hard against the wall,
Then it would bounce and shatter in the fall.
Smiling, she would stand, waiting in the hall,

Sometimes she could time me, and catch a fly ball!
We had a brand-new, two-bedroom,
Brick-bungalow home,
No backyard fences,
I was able to wander off and roam.
My poor Mother spent
A lot of time hunting,
Because at every chance,
I would take off running.

Men came and installed
That most hated
Restraining, incarcerating
Cyclone Fence.
Right up one side
And down the other I went.

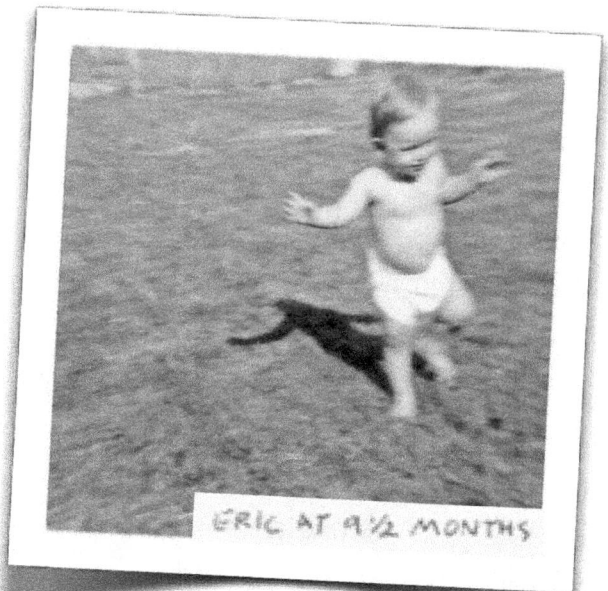

ERIC AT 9 ½ MONTHS

But sometimes that was
Not quite enough,
Going down the other side,
I would catch my pant cuff.
I would scream bloody murder,
Hanging there upside down,
My Mother would come running,
With a laugh, then a frown.
Then sternly she would tell me
To quit acting the clown.

I went to my friends,
Who lived two- and three-doors down,
Danny and Greggy,
A closely-bound friendship we'd found.
And every morning we would run out
And just play around.
Rain and snow often came,
And some days I would miss,
But my early young years,
Were filled with happiness and bliss.

Being a toddler in the Fifties,
Was so extremely enjoyable.
Quite often we got in trouble;
We were told to mind the Golden Rule.
We were thinking that a Golden Ruler
Would be downright pretty cool.
Everything was ecstatically fun,
And life was so very beautiful.

Then my reality crashed,
And my planets collided,
I could not be assuaged, mollified,
Not even incited.
No one had forewarned me,
It was so heartless and cruel,
When my Mom dressed me up
For My First Day Of School!

THE MINNESOTA ICEMAN COMMETH
PART I

In the Spring of 1969,
It was for us, a most frustrating time;
Larry and I were just sitting around wishing;
Two teenage outdoorsy young guys,
Who wanted to do nothing but fishing,
We were seriously preparing to graduate,
Drinking stolen beer, down in our basement Man Cave.
Throwing darts at the board on the wall,
We were heeding the Northwest call,
To escape this suburban, well-ordered place.

Argosy, the best magazine of all,
Said that an Abominable Snowman, a Yeti
Would soon be coming to our shopping mall.
From way up on high in the Himalayas,
Was where they claimed, he had been slain.
But the Northern Minnesota forest,
Is where he was most likely found.
That was where he had really died
And fallen facedown to the ground.

A fictitious story, was created to disguise,
The true place of origin, of his recent demise.
The Feds wanted to abscond with the Beast,
But the owner said "Not in the very least!"
"I must show it to one and to all,
In all of the major cities'
Brand-new Shopping Malls."

12

From Milwaukee to Chicago,
To the Motor City he came,
In a semi-tractor trailer,
To begin his Celebrity Claim To Fame.

In a thick, refrigerated glass box,
Mounted four feet off of the floor,
We spent our seven dollars and fifty cents,
And entered into the trailer's back door.
He was stunning to see, our eyes witnessed a feast,
Gazing down upon, this most incredible Beast.
He was frozen 4-8" inches deep, in a layer of ice,
And he had recently been shot, in his chest and his eye.

Still, he had managed to fall forward,
Then landed in the water on his face,
Blood drained down, about four inches,
Crimson was instantly frozen in place.

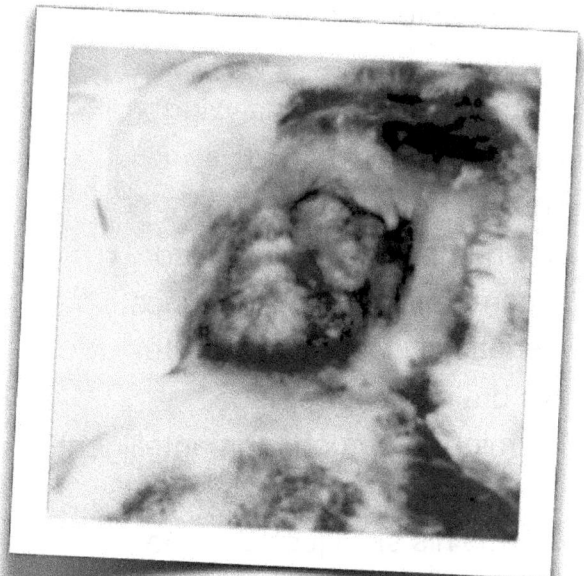

Larry and I were both exactly six-foot-four,
As we lay next to the Beast on the floor;
We gauged he was about seven feet tall,
Maybe just a few inches more, close call!

He was massive and solid, not flabby like a bear,
We guessed 600 pounds minimally, just to be fair.
As recently-trained students of Taxidermy classes,
We brought along with us, our big magnifying glasses.

The hair follicle test,
The Great Beast easily passes,
We were definitely convinced
He was not made of waxes!
We wondered if he was
The Anthropologist's true Missing Link,
And we wondered,
How much when alive,
Did he actually stink?

I remember while analyzing
His face and his head,
He was not ape-like at all,
Nor human-like, but instead
A completely-original species,
Genetically incommensurate,
His brain could be huge,
He might be much more intelligent.

Or was his skull just all bone,
Mentally a slow starter?
14

What an incredible tale to tell,
We spent all of three hours.
His face was rectangular-shaped,
Very original, incomparable;
I had no reference at all,
With which to make it relatable.

We tried to tell our family and friends,
They said we were foolish and demented,
Instead, not very long after,
Our new-found Beast Friend,
Packed up the trailer and suddenly and left town,
Heading for the city of the Cleveland Browns,
Just a short distance by Lake Erie, down south.

Last seen on the highway,
To Ohio he was bound,
But he just disappeared.
Both he and the trailer,
Have never been found.

THE MINNESOTA ICEMAN COMMETH
PART II

During this year of 2016,
I have been daydreaming and deliberating,
As to why the Smithsonian Institution,
Makes all of the remnants of Giants disappear.

During this year's Holiday Season,
I have been reminiscing, reflecting,
Contemplating, trying to reason,
As to where the Iceman has gone missing—
Long gone for the past 47 years.

I recently find, to my most pleasant surprise,
That there exists the Museum of the Weird,
Where the replica of the Beast is still frozen in ice.
Way down south in good old ol' Austin, Texas,
Where the owner, Steve Busti, has kept this story alive!

This revelation finds me very grateful,
And personally I am most satisfied,
Contented, overwhelmed and beholden,
Relieved and indebted, very much obliged!

In 1974 a scientific book was written,
About this Brutish Frozen Fellow,
With a detailed, in-depth description,
By a preeminent zoologist from Belgium,
The distinguished Dr. Bernard Heuvelmans.

The title is "Neanderthal," subtitled
"The Strange Saga of the Minnesota Iceman."

He studied The Beast in the very good company
Of the famous American journalist, who also
Was the naturalist on The Garry Moore Show;
Ivan T. Sanderson, was the Jungle Jim of the Sixties.

It was the month of December in 1968,
In northern Minnesota; for the next three busy days,
They measured, photographed and made annotations,
They wrote copious amounts of detailed observations,
And they illustrated their most meticulous examinations.

The men had taken
A rigorous and scrutinizing good look,
And after five years
It became Hauvelmans' outstanding book.
It was exposing to the world
This groundbreaking biography,
But it fell on the deaf ears
Of the Scientific Community!

Because this hairy, Humongous Beast,
Long gone, he was no longer to be seen;
He had just evaporated into very thin air;
Mysteriously, he had just up and disappeared!

The prestigious Scientific Society,
Secure with their Grants and their Tenure,
From their comfortable, overstuffed armchairs,
Reading their mainstream newspapers,
It was so much simpler to just blindly refute;
With hubris they were so 'enlightened and astute!'

They claimed that Doctor Heuvelmans
Had been dishonestly deceived and duped
By a cunning backwoodsman, a crafty impersonator,
A carnival showman, a most audacious entertainer!
Frank D. Hansen, the enterprising owner,
Was caught between the proverbial rock
And an unlawfully, illegally-serious hard spot.

He was in the personal possession
Of a creature that he had recently just got,

18

That had most obviously been murdered;
At least two times he had been shot.

Hansen's first claim was that he had shipped it,
And had exported it all the way here from Asia;
But he found out later that it would be a violation,
Of the United States and its laws of importation.

In Hollywood he had some studio friends,
They created for him an artistic replacement,
Not yet knowing as to what purpose or end,
The replica was made for a future engagement.
Studio artists, using only their studio imagination,
Not having viewed this unique genetic formation,
Constructed sight unseen, a conceptualized fabrication.

But Frank D. Hansen did not care at all
About those burdensome biological details;
It was made as an emergency substitute.
It was his forensic legal loophole surrogate;
A makeshift, counterfeit, fraudulent, pseudo-alternate.
Creating a hasty, spur-of-the-moment replica,
A creation that was visually inaccurate.
His new plan was to claim that the real Beast was a fake,
In case the authorities wanted to confiscate,
To commandeer his exhibit of the real Creature,
In what the government proclaims "to appropriate."

This opened the door for the spineless critics,
For the timid and overly-pretentious pundits;
Not a shred of curiosity to witness for themselves.

Scientific pretenders, lackadaisical scientists,
Resting on their monthly Grants and Entitlements.

Then some of the more sensitive types started whining.
They said Hansen may have in his personal possession,
Possibly a deformed or maybe a mutated human being,
That could be a victim of some murderous transgression.
The authorities decided auspiciously
That they needed to have an official autopsy;
Confused and bewildered as to what they were seeing,
Observing what they were viewing, but still not believing.

Back in March of 1969,
Being cautious, my friend Larry and I
Clearly had no intention of being hustled,
Easily bamboozled or swindled.
We were going to make absolutely sure
That we were going to get our full money's worth;
Ticket prices were a hefty seven and a half bucks.
Mr. Hansen, while watching, had casually told us,
That his next move was taking the show on to Cleveland;
But later on he just disappeared, he never showed up.

According to Bernard Heuvelmans' rendition,
That I have taken from his unacknowledged book,
Hansen went on a tour of the Canadian Northland,
I suspect to get away from those covert spooks,
Those cloak-and-dagger, secret-agent Americans,
Who still wanted to take possession of his Bigfoot.
Assuming Fred Hansen was now trapped in Canada,
While he was trying to get back into Minnesota,

20

This is where Hansen and the amazing Creature
Must have been stopped at the United States border.
This is where they were eventually held up;
They had nothing left to do but surrender,
They had nothing left to do but give up.

Hansen was called on the phone on March 25th,
By Marlise Simons, of "The Times of London."
He repeated that "Because of unfavorable publicity,
From now on, only a model will be shown to the public,
Rather than the real creature."
Which was noticeably now missing on this day;
Somehow mysteriously, it had been whisked away.

It is only my own personal assumption,
That instead of going to Cleveland at all,
Hansen and the real Minnesota Iceman
Crossed over or under the Detroit River,
Traversing the border into Windsor, Canada,
To avoid a Federal surreptitious abduction,
A government arrest, a judicial confiscation.
Driving counterclockwise around Michigan,
Inexpertly trying to avoid observation,
I am sure the Canadian Mounted Police,
Always knew his itinerary and his destination.

Purportedly the alerted U.S. authorities were waiting
To nab this precocious man and his unusual cadaver,
Before they would admit him back into his nation.
He had to give up the Sasquatch in his possession,
If he wanted to cross at the Minnesota border station.

Back at his home in northern Minnesota,
To the Press, Hansen did publicly state,
That his mysterious and undisclosed partner,
Recently came to recover and confiscate,
To repossess and retake his personal estate.
Then the Beast was concealed and sequestered,
Far away in a covert and clandestine place.

At first Hansen claimed his patron was Vietnamese.
Then he was a Russian entrepreneur, then a Chinese.
Claimed it was an anonymous movie producer;
He was hastily making up exotic stories,
Then inexplicably changed his narrative once again.

Since then this incredibly invaluable creature,
Has completely vanished for many decades.
For ages he has mysteriously gone missing,
Still to this day, he is completely unknown,
As to where he was taken and relocated;
We are now, at this juncture, just guessing!

I think the Feds gave Hansen two options:
To spend the rest of his days in prison,
Or to pretend that this all never happened.
Into his country, they would let him back in,
Free to exhibit, and to still make some money,
Showing everyone his unsubstantiated replica;
People not ever realizing or comprehending
What it was actually that they saw.

In my suspicious, always-questioning opinion,
It is my amateurish, astute speculation,
That the creature was then loaded up on a military gyro,
And flown to Wright-Patterson Air Force Base in Ohio.
That surreptitious space, that underground place,
Where they like to keep amorphous specimens,
Aberrations and mutations from the human race;
All of those weird and very strange sorts of things.
Where out of the public eye are kept unusual beings,
Because we the people, the uneducated masses,
Are too 'vulnerable' and 'childishly defenseless;'
Just immature pubescent whining adolescents.

That is their bogus excuse to always deny publicly,
Any unusual or very strange mysterious critters,
Any amazing discovery that is a scientific anomaly.
Corporate religion and government surveillance
Feel that your need to know is not really necessary!

So now this interesting tale is Ancient History,
But it is real and exists, I personally guarantee;
Saving this chronicle was very important to me.
If anyone tells you there is no Sasquatch, no Bigfoot,
Now you can tell them this story—the inside scoop—
That it really did happen, I am telling the truth!

An obituary for Bernard Heuvelmans (1916-2001)
can be found online at:
lorencoleman.com/bernard_heuvelmans_obituary.html

Family

BLACK SHEEP

How pleasantly warm, to be part of a family.
A necessity of life, as basic as gravity.
Such a glorious blessing,
I cannot emphasize enough.
The heartfelt, pleasant feelings
I must confess of Family Love.
But alas, a Black Sheep
From the herd must be shoved.

Sometimes a Bad Apple
Will make us all grapple.
Resolutions drumming just like strumming fingers,
Emotional damage still festers and lingers.

Plucking at our intimate heartstrings
Is most destructive,
Sibling malevolence
Makes decisions imperative,
It necessitates difficult
Cohesive reckoning,
Reviewing extremely painful
Tough family choices.
Angry fists waving
With detrimental, strident voices;
Memories of disunion,
The sting is still lingering.

The selfish or individual role
Cannot be allowed to divide up the whole.
The Family must make the demanding choices,
To expel or repel,
The schismatic mole,
Or the problematic troll;
It can be incredibly painful
To everyone's soul.

Yet in unity, undivided,
The Clan ebulliently rejoices!
Yet forgets and forgives,
And let lives,
In nonjudgmental voices.

FAITH

Faith has the grace
And the prettiest face
Of all the young ladies
Near that Tri-Cities place.

She easily takes the Blue Ribbon
As the World's Sweetest Niece.
A beautiful young lady,
Who always says "please."

Such a sweet disposition,
All the family agrees!

MY BEAUTIFUL, LOVING WIFE

She eternally has been, my sole Kindred Spirit.
Always indulging me in my artistic endeavors.
Choosing ideas, that for us, have some merit.
Always supports me, even in rough, stormy weather.

Such a blessing to have a trustworthy companion,
As I become older, all wrinkled and weathered;
For so many years we have traveled in tandem,
For so many years, we have journeyed together.

I would barely exist,
Living all alone in my life,
Without the one who has loved me,
Without my wonderful Wife.

Her unwavering attention,
Her steadfast affection,
That intelligent girl,
With the sexy allure.

Who has created for me,
Such a safe place to be,
Without stressful strife,
Such a comfortable life!

MY DEVOTED LOVING MOTHER

My dear, loving Mother
Peacefully passed away yesterday;
I thought I was emotionally ready,
But my grief still perseveres today.

I hold my highest esteem for her,
Above any other;
That beautiful woman,
Who was my dear, loving Mother.

She was always there for me,
To wipe the tears from my face;
She would hold me and hug me,
Taking me back to that happy place.

Born in 1928, she was
The youngest of the three sisters;
Christened Emily Henrietta,
In Dearborn's St. Alphonsus Church.

Uprooted when she was only about three,
She was relocated to Aschaffenburg, Germany;
She had an idyllic European childhood,
But her teenage years were spent surviving World War II.

Hiding in basements
From bombs falling in droves;
Three times she was bombed,

Right out of her own home.

They moved out to a farmhouse in the country,
But the girls all alone would have to hitchhike
Riding on military troop transports to school,
They had no other choice, they no longer had bikes.

They got tired of waiting at the crossroads,
And decided to walk alone on their own,
Then only a few minutes later,
The crossroads completely exploded
Into a giant, fifty-foot crater.

She lost two boyfriends, one to the SS,
And one was to a bomb, hiding in the basement.
She was often trapped in bomb shelters
There was nothing left, no choices for her.

In 1946, the U.S. refused to
Let her return to her homeland.
She was kept under a dark cloud,
Of suspicion and mistrust,
Where she worked for only food rations,
Translating for the American Military
Also with her Father and two Sisters,
Deciphering important German documents.

Finally she was permitted,
Then eventually admitted,
For American repatriation,
And eventually, assimilation.

But it was not very easy to adjust,
To a different culture and language.
Where she had been inauspiciously born,
Next to the River Rouge Ford Plant,
Very nearly two decades before.
It was Henry Ford's second city,
In Detroit's suburb of Dearborn.
Her strong German accent
Was her saddened fate,
Surviving and socializing with
Those that were still full of hate.

She taught me the principle
That it was not Christian to hate,
Even if uneducated people,
Were horrid towards her,
Acting rudely and in bad taste.

"Always remember," she would say,
"That God wants you to ingratiate,
No matter how much
You have been offended by hate."

This rule that she required of me,
It was terribly difficult to tolerate;
Because when I've been wronged,
I usually preferred to obliterate.

Control your temper,
In hate do not participate;
Because of her teachings,

I am still alive at this date.

Like Jesus always forgiving others
For unacceptable behavior,
She was not only a Saint on this earth,
She was also my loving Savior!

MY WONDERFUL BABY BOY

Like a car tunnel that cuts
Through a huge redwood tree,
That is the size of the hole
That was bored through my heart.
There has been nothing more tragic,
Nor so painful to me,
Than to experience my Son
Prematurely depart.

He was red-headed and six feet five inches tall,
Two hundred and forty-five pounds, and very lean;
He was a stronger and taller version of me.

I was a Weekend Dad, right from the start.
But there was never enough time, you see,
To properly fulfill my parenting part.

I was working long hours,
Had a new wife and two babies.
I was always so tired,
And we spent too much time apart.

He died from an accidental overdose,
An excessive amount of too much alcohol.
In hopes of a hangover cure, he chose,
One Dilaudid pill; it became his downfall.

The doctor said that when he went to bed

He lay down approximately around 2 AM;
By 3 AM he was stone cold — he was dead.

I will never see,
My beautiful child again.
What a Gift from God, a Joy;
A Blessing he was from the start.

I grieve so deeply, I weep
Over my broken promises,
And so many more maybes
That I will never be able to keep.

PARTNER FOR LIFE, MY WIFE

She, unknowingly, is sometimes a distraction,
To my literary pursuits, my artistic endeavors.
Such a lovely and loyal, trustworthy companion,
As I become wrinkled, and even more textured.
Partners in travel, no more highway isolation,
We have explored and journeyed so well together.

Enjoying a great marriage,
While wearing our rings,
She is well organized,
And she packs everything;
If she fails to remember
To bring anything,
I'm available to blame,
For not listening!

Of our personal items, we are prudent and prepared;
Our logistical planning mistakes are unusually rare.
Sharing flavorful foreign cuisine, tasty ethnic food fare,
Dining becomes an adventure, that together we share.

Her fresh Margaritas so exquisitely fine,
With Grand Marnier, so deliciously divine.
Add fresh, tasty limes, it's difficult to decline;
Discretion is what is, more than likely prescribed.
I need to practice personal poise and restraint,
Measure most carefully how much to inebriate.

A loving partner,
A most faithful bride,
She has been steadfast,
Evermore by my side.
With whom intimately
I can always confide,
On whom faithfully,
I have always relied.
Tears of joy, shared together,
We have many times cried,
Lots of really good times;
It's been a wonderful ride!

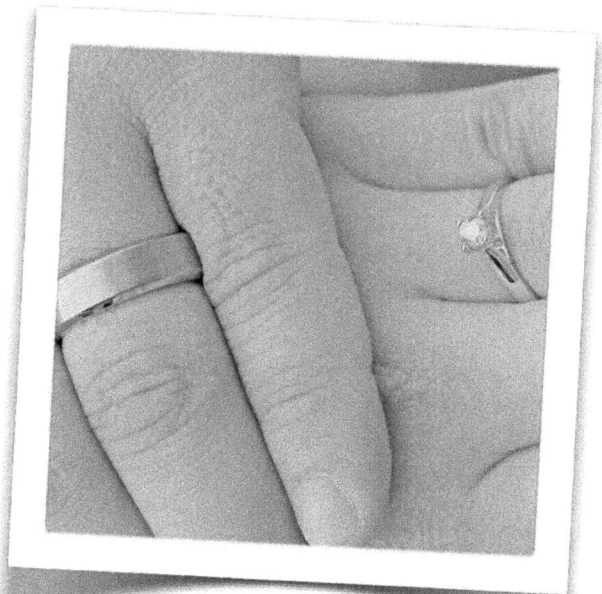

RETROSPECTIVE REMINISCENCES

Leaning back on the kitchen counter rather leisurely,
While drinking my freshly-made Coffee Nudge,
Displayed is a picture window of our family history.
The fridge now becomes my personal Judge.

Gazing on a collection of vacation magnets,
A diversified mixture of a tchotchkes collage,
A billboard of our sabbatical diversions;
Of many day trips and some week-long excursions,
A mishmash, an assortment, a total hodgepodge.

Family tours, good times, souvenir finds, long lines!
It says to me I did a good job, as a Father this time,
Before God, I envision that I carried my load,
And that I led my family on down the right road!

SHE CARES

She cares about the plight
Of lost cats and sick dogs;
And it so breaks her heart,
How they harvest the hogs.

She has taken a personal stance
Against those rendering plants,
Those butchering stainless-steel processors,
Carving up our born-free, wild-range horses.

Cows and turkeys and chickens,
All that hormone needle-sticking;
Fed nothing but Genetically-Modified Organisms,
By those nefarious, vile Corporate Biotech Forces.

She has empathy for the trees,
Tearful sympathy for the bees,
She is all about the wolves and the bears;
Wants to protect the Wilderness everywhere.

She does all of this because she so genuinely cares;
For future generations, she just wishes to share.
Very soon this sensitive, caring young lady,
Before long, she may not be very much alive;
Because she just won't stop her cell phone texting,
While she blindly continues to carelessly drive.

SUMMER LILY

I have witnessed the radiant shine
Of such natural beauty sublime.
Always here, by my side, every year,
Warms my heart, gives me comfort from tears.

Her presence accentuates the wine,
When we sit down together and dine.
To the indubitably, discerning eye,
A lovely flower so pleasingly fine.

A radiant vision of beauty,
Standing next to my bed,
The scent of spring flowers,
Wafting through the air by my head.
Soft and smooth to the touch,
Not enough can be said,
A blossom of loveliness;
Such a splendid woman I've wed.

Life

BY OUR OWN DESIGN

Three times Mankind has almost died;
That is recently-discovered scientific history.
Maybe it was because the gods were defied,
Because *Homo Erectus* was created for slavery,
By the Ashkenazi 400,000 years ago,
In South Africa just for mining their gold.
Yahweh, the one and only true God that we know,
Was enraged by the artificial, genetic mutations;
What the demigods had done, to all of his Creation.

Human bodies attached,
To the heads of birds,
Human genes crossed
With a wide range of various animals;
Such a calamitous construct.
From the Animal Kingdom's
Full variety of feathered flocks,
Freaks of nature, half human.
Even the omniscient Creator,
Not surprisingly, was a bit shocked!

From Bovine to Equine to Canine and Feline,
Crocodilian, Falconine, even Corvine,
Leonine to Lupine,
Serpentine and Ursine, Hircine,
Elephantine, Porcine, and Asinine.

Extraterrestrial, self-declared, mini-gods
Creating giants and cross-bred monsters;
Robbing the planet of its valuable gold,
Just a bunch of Interplanetary Mobsters.

Yahweh was crestfallen,
Disappointed, downhearted;
He was angry at all of the damage
That was done to human blood.
He forever banished them;
All of the Invaders departed.
He wiped away a tear,
And brought to his Creation,
The most devastating, Noah's Flood.

The Earth had received
A most thorough cleansing,
And all of our history,
Had been buried deeply in mud.
The animals and people,
Embarked from the Ark, singing.
In rich soil, planting seeds,
That were quickly beginning to bud.

This was the time that domestic grains
And farm animals appeared;
God gave Man new genetic creations
For replenishing the Earth.
He was protecting Mankind;
No longer could Alien Invaders interfere.
The human condition had changed,

We were going through a Major Rebirth.

Banished from the Kingdom of Heaven,
The Devil Incarnate fell down from the sky.
He could not physically appear,
But he could easily mess with your mind.
For Mankind it was a provocation
That we had no choice but to defy.
Protecting one's soul from evil
Was the new challenge defined.

The edict was simple: honor God,
Just be Good, just be Kind.
But Satan seduced half of the people,
Unrelentingly, time after time.
God said,"Honor my Creation,
And it is life after death that you will find.
If not, then that sinful Serpent,
Will make you pay for your crimes!"

After a few thousand years,
Civilization began to revive.
First were the Sumerians, and then
The Egyptians began to thrive.
Throughout all of the continents,
Mankind began to expand.
Humanity bred so prolifically,
Now today there is a shortage of land.

Incredibly, we did inexplicably well for ourselves,
Populations continued to expand.

But we no longer could handle aggression, starvation,
Not even our most minimal of issues.
Things generally escalated out of control,
Desperately, most awfully, quite out of hand!
Beelzebub keeps winning the battles for souls,
While weeping eyes are rapidly soaking up tissues.

Mankind has become self absorbed in himself,
As he is running out of time.
He is committing suicide by Earth,
Forcing our Mother, to scrape off the slime.
The insatiable greed of a few,
Is bringing our Planet to its knees.
We better start begging, like James Brown singing,
"Please, please, please, please, please!"

So there you have it,
We have created our own Demise.
We've tolerated evil behavior,
Stealing and murder and lies.
It is time to stand tall for Justice,
And what is morally right.
Way far too many of you,
Have already given up the fight.

This time we have created our own Extinction,
By our own design.
I can only hope God comes to the rescue,
And saves Humanity in time!

HEALTH IS WEALTH

Would you desire to make a healthy self-improvement?
It facilitates and eases that morning bowel movement.
That doesn't take any money, and it really does work;
It will benefit all of your body, it has many perks.
It cleanses your liver, and kidneys and intestines,
It will keep you eternally, internally-pristine!

Cleverly simple, so very important you try it,
It is famously called the Japanese Water Diet.
Get yourself two 16-ounce water bottles,
Refrigerate them overnight, so they get very cold.
And when you awake, take them to the commode.
Guzzle them down, finish both water bottles.
It frees up your body, so you can now hit the road.

It is better than a cup of coffee in the mornings;
Best of all there's no need, for creepy health warnings.
Especially if you are sensitive to caffeine,
Or you cannot risk going for a long walk,
To avoid a personally-embarrassing scene.
I am so glad that we could have this little talk.

HOT SHOWERS

Awakening a stiff body, with a rock-heavy head,
I am barely arising, trying to get up from my bed.
I can hardly distinguish, my eyes are blood red,
My neck has developed a pulled muscle, I dread.
The tendons in my shoulders and lower back ache,
In places long ago, that had previous breaks;
I am now paying the price for my prior mistakes.
Old sports injuries, these pains, I just wish to escape!

Vertebrae are making those arthritic clicks.
They sound like the breaking of dry little sticks.
Deep, painful twinges from inside of my bones,
In Old Age, we often suffer in silence, alone.
What I so instantly do require—
What I most sincerely do desire—
Hot steam is to what, I really do aspire!

Usually when I am feeling especially dour,
Awakening in that crisp, early-morning hour,
When the temperature is dropping much lower,
I want an eye-opening, hot, steaming shower!

Pulsating force, high-pressure water jets,
Pounding down upon my back and neck;
From the top of my head, to my feet on the deck.
There arises an ecstatic, tingling sensation,
A quivering shiver runs right down my spine.
It melts and dissolves all of my body's frustrations,
My heart and my soul, once again, have aligned!

LOVE

When you spy that special someone
Who really catches your eye,
You position yourself to be noticed,
And then you walk casually nearby.

As you make up your excuses,
And start some clever conversation,
Hearing the sound of their voice
Creates that tingling sensation.

Your eyes then get lost
In those deep, dark, liquid pools,
They just keep on sparkling,
Like rare, precious jewels.

Some laughter and compliments,
Deep breaths and white smiles,
The hair, the shoulders,
The legs, and the hips,
It all completely beguiles.

Your heart expands like a balloon
And it wants to burst with desire,
All you want is to hold and to hug,
Just to contain all that fire.
With twinkling eyes,
I am so happily ecstatic for you,
For apparently now,

Your love has become very true.
That no one is needed
To give you a push or a shove,
It seems you have fallen hopelessly,
Helplessly, so deeply in love.

Like the clouds and the breezes,
Flowing far up above,
That makes your heart soar,
On the wings of a dove.
You can be very assured,
That you have found your true love.

NOSTALGIA

There once was a day that I could be
The way I like to remember me.
I had the strength and the energy
For what is now, those years times three.

I reminisce much more now, as I become old,
As the days pass on by, and the crystal nights glow.
Wherefrom do they come, where to and fro,
Where do they go, I do not really know.

As my life starts to fade slowly down the road,
I am now less of the seeker.
As I grow older and weaker,
Now my soul has begun to carry my load.

As I go longer and longer,
With resolve and conviction,
It evolves with distinction;
Better election of direction.
Better choices, restrained voices,
A conscious decision, of a positive vision.
No fears of derision, no more moral collisions,
No more conflicts of right and wrong.

Why keep on singing the same old sad song?
Conjecturing when I will be moving along.
As I get older, the more my heart becomes strong,
I have ascertained the future, where I think I belong.

54

SINS OF JONATHAN LIVINGSTON

Nature has its own agenda, that it wants to display;
Seagulls will happily take flight, up our hill today.
They do not come for pleasure, not to stay nor to play;
They have one single mission, they plan to enter the fray.

When they leave their seaside habitat,
You cannot win against these flying rats!
Nature always adapts in every way;
Up here, it's Trash-Can-Garbage Day!

Folks that forget to fasten their lids tight,
Set themselves up for a disturbing sight.
These big flying birds will cause embarrassing distress,
Spreading around rubbish, making such a public mess!

Then the crows move on in,
Swirling around like Arabic Jinn,
Creating a tumultuous din.
Fasten those lids, or you cannot win!

All of your garbage scattered,
In front of your house,
In the morning your neighbors,
View it when barely aroused.
The birds turn your rubbish,
Into a frightening sight,
The neighborhood can see,
What you had for dinner last night!

SUMMERTIME

I do so love those warm and sultry ways,
During summer's hot and humid days.
Those stay-late-in-bed, cool, breezy mornings,
Golden beams flowing, like a raiment adorning.

Springtime is the season of rebirth and trust;
While summertime becomes a forest fire of lust.
The rays of the sun, begin warming my skin,
The cold water shocks me, when I go for a swim.

Songbirds and butterflies,
Glide and float on the wind,
Sweet scents of fine barbecue,
So good it's a sin.
The hiss of a bottle opener,
Uncapping a cold beer.
Motorcycling along,
As a hot breeze whips through my hair.

Rushing to eat ice cream,
Melting all over my hands,
While watching a baseball game,
From above, in the stands.
Looking forward to visiting,
Lots of family and friends,
Traveling on vacations,
In many scenic new lands.

Now I am older, I sit and idly meditate,
On faces with forgotten names, at this late of a date.
I inwardly ruminate, and genuinely speculate,
Not knowing at all, of their eventual fates.

I'm thankful for love,
Happily I have had more than my share,
Passionate romance,
And spontaneous summer affairs.
Peacefully reminiscing,
So absorbed, quite unawares,
Sipping bourbon and relaxing,
In my old rocking chair.

THE BALLAD OF WINE CRIMES OF NATURE

Is that the sink?
I think it stinks!
My frustration level
Is on the brink.
What should I do?
I've got to think!

Fruit flies are all buzzing about,
So annoying, even a small amount.
Black specks floating, stress me out;
It really makes me want to shout!

Tragically they die, limply floating in my wine,
It is not their malicious plan or design.
They just like to get drunk, most all of the time,
While singing Frat House drinking songs that rhyme!

My wine can no longer, be described as fine,
On very fresh, raw meat, I do not wish to dine.
Romance is no longer, ambient and sublime,
I am going to commit, a Heinous Insect Crime!

You can try to run the hot water a while,
But those fly eggs will still survive and beguile.
They will just barely, oh so rarely, be riled;
Angrily, I wish to destroy and defile.

Adding some Drano, to soften the scum just a little.
Declare war on the fruit flies, it is time now to settle.
I really want to get going, get feisty and mettle,
I am going to fill up, the Big Rusty Tea Kettle.

Then waiting around, for that whistling sound,
Boiling water is the best treatment that I have found;
Then into the drain, steaming-hot, pour it on down.
We tip back a few drinks, and make toasts all around!

Please leave your used lemon and lime rinds,
Grind in the disposal, to leave their essence behind.
To your relatives and friends, be so very kind,
Leave their aromatic senses, and taste buds refined.

TRUST

You spend your whole childhood
Learning about trust.
When considering marriage,
It must be discussed.

Some make decisions,
Just based on their lust;
Some guys are just looking,
For that perfectly-shaped bust.

And both sexes think
A first-rate ass is a must;
Some things are not perfect,
Sometimes you have to adjust.

Of sex and of money,
There can be no mistrust,
If you don't want a marriage,
That will crumble into dust.
Carefully choose the one who is worthy,
One who is uncommonly honest and just!

Miscellaneous

CHRISTMAS LETTER

This year we've been resting,
And just empty nesting.
Bought some new cell phones,
But still only texting.
The kids have moved out,
But still within a loud shout,
We are so happy having them,
Near and about.

We took two vacations,
Because keeping in touch,
To see our relations,
Is what matters so much.
Three years I'm retired,
Writing, feeling inspired;
Lisa's still working,
An amount she desires.

We go to second-hand stores,
And estate sales shopping,
Sunday dinners and barbecues,
Routine never stopping.
We planted the garden,
Growing plenty of food,
Harvesting Nature's rich bounty,
For our own good.

Enjoying movies from Netflix,
We watch them together,

A lot of big-screen TV,
During wet, wintry weather.
Occasionally, we go cruising
And exploring all around,
Interesting places we've discovered,
Just recently found
On the most visually-pleasing,
People-popular Puget Sound.

As we get older,
And a little bit dizzy,
Our routine life, happily,
Does keep us busy.
We want you all to know,
When comes the winter snows,
We will be cozy and warm,
When the Fat Man shows!

DO YOU DREAM CITY?

So many, many years ago,
Having lived in San Francisco,
I would get this recurring dream,
Every now and again, it seemed.

I would be exiting from the Freeway,
Near the wharf called The Embarcadero,
When—I don't know why—I would lose control,
Breaking through the guardrail, going into a roll.

Crashing onto the dark roof of a building,
All of my senses were spinning and reeling.
Pulling myself through the shattered car window
I manage to extricate my body and go.

Building by building, at least five stories high,
Making my exit by means of the fire escapes.
But I keep bumping into drunken sleeping bums,
Stinking of old sweat and cheap vodka and rum.

They rise up to confront me, intimidating.
It all may to you sound very silly,
But I start throwing them willy-nilly,
Over the hand railings, their bodies go sailing.
In the dark duskiness
I'm heaving two or three in a row,
Flung down to the dirty concrete streets,
Very far down below.

This same story repeating
Over and over methinks,
Would most probably, be easily
Analyzed by a Shrink.

I later headed north
To the Emerald City.
No longer recurring,
After a very long period of time,
I stopped having my dream
Of throwing bums without pity.

And I started a new one—
An adventure with a bit of a climb.
On Capitol Hill it starts out
In sidewalk-wide alleys at night.
I creep under overhanging Clematis
And long, stringy vines,
Avoiding muggers
And bad-looking street-thug sluggers.
On concrete stair flights,
Carefully wending my way down
To the tropical, swamp-like shores
Of Lake Washington.

"Hey, hey, what did you say?"
I know! How could this be?
It's much more like Florida's
Lake Okeechobee.
Loaded with spiders, hungry alligators,

And slithering snakes,
And the path is so narrow and so close,
To the edge of the lake.

I have to jump very quickly,
And be light on my feet,
Avoiding lighting-quick,
Aggressive gator strikes,
Dodging vicious snakes,
And poisonous spider bites.
For my very next challenge
I must climb this mountainous hill,
I make it to the top of the peak,
But my passage is nil.

A gargantuan-wide chute
Of deep, rushing water,
Much too massive to cross,
I must hike down and around,
To the place Downtown,
Where the water goes underground.

After this I head north,
My new direction is found,
Till I see that first bus stop,
All the way out of town.

And that is where
This unusual dream ends,
On a park pew,
Watching the glowing sun set.

Every single time,
Sitting on this bench I am found
Just north of Seattle,
On a solitary hilltop.
I am sitting alone
At an isolated bus stop,
Watching a setting sun,
From up above the Puget Sound.

Now I am putting it out there,
To all the rest of you,
Maybe you are many,
Or maybe you are just a few.
Would you care to satisfy my curiosity?
Do tell me, of these dangerous confrontations,
Should I be pitied,
Or do you also experience
Myriad trips through Dream City?

HAIRFORCE, OF COURSE!

If your hair is starting to look like hay,
Or maybe your roots are turning to gray,
Do not while away, or waste another day,
You can look very glamorous, right away!

Go downtown to Rucker Street,
Two lovely ladies that you will meet,
Ann and Mindi, who will happily greet,
With smiling faces, they are so sweet.

Luckily for you, if you cannot afford to pay,
The girls might let you barter your debt away.
If you have some special materials or skills,
They possibly may bargain, to reduce your bill.

So pick yourself up and quickly get down to their place,
To the building downtown, with that big smiley face.
Improve your appearance, please do not be a disgrace,
Get a coiffure that will be a Blue Ribbon-First Place!

HAMBURGER ASSASSINATION

Hot-headed Ronald McDonald
Tragically did a very bad thing.
It was a show stopper;
It was quite a Whopper.

He brutally shot down the Burger King,
And his splendidly-wonderful wife,
The elegantly-statuesque Dairy Queen,
Blatantly right in front of Five Guys.

The deceased royal couple
Had publicly disclosed
That Wendy, his redheaded girlfriend,
Was looking excessively Fat.

The funeral services have been set;
They will be held at the White Castle.
And it is most tastefully catered by
Our very own illustrious Burger Chef.

We all plan to be
In-N-Out very quickly,
At sub-Sonic speed,
Lickety-split in a Jiffy.

We'll have plenty of time
To visit Bob's brother, Jack,
Who lives in a Box,
Next door to the Shack.

HAPPY BIRTHDAY

Happy Birthday to you,

May all your hopes and dreams come true.

May you never again be blue.

May all of your family and friends

Forever keep loving you!

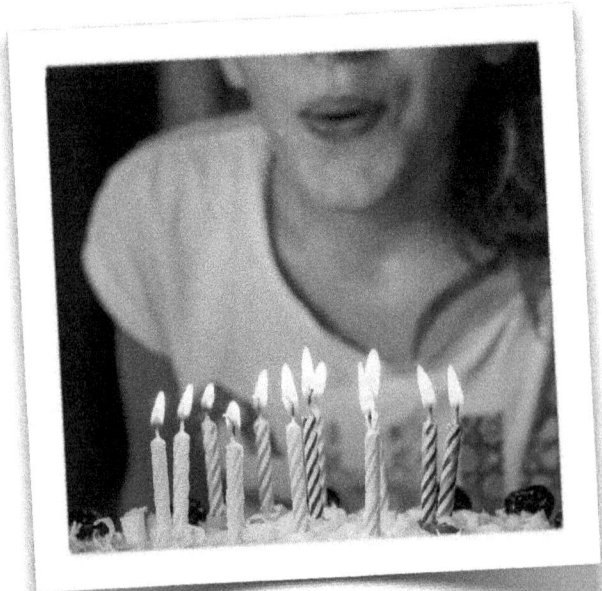

HELGA'S RIVERSIDE TAVERN

Ten miles from the mouth
Of the mighty Snohomish River,
There lies, what long ago used to be,
A historical logging mill town.
Today it has spread out;
Most of the forests have gone urban,
But on First Street, down by the river,
There's a hearty pub we have found.

On weekends, the kids get
Ice cream cones and balloons.
Lots of stops, antiques shops,
Restaurants and saloons.
A park by the water,
Farmer's Markets, parades,
The Appliance Recycle,
The Airport, and trains.

But the best spot around town,
My most favorite place,
Is Helga's Riverside Tavern,
Because the food's really great!

Visiting this place is a pleasure,
Just to walk down the old streets.
All of the folks living here,
Are exceptionally sweet;
And that, in and of itself,

Is a much-appreciated treat.
But the best part of this place,
That sends up all the cheers,
Is their excellent selection
Of our local craft beers!

SEXXX

Sex is the very best
Of all the pleasures in life.
I have managed to put
Many things to the test;
Oh, please believe me,
How much I have tried.

Some have gross gluttonous
Capacious penchants for food.
The flush of the gambling rush
Will get some addictively hooked.
And some have a hefty propensity
For alcohol that is overly consumed.
And some just have too vast a partiality
For dangerous drugs, too amply abused.

But what the larger majority of us require,
Who are the human collective conglomerated,
People exuding strong emotions on fire,
With passions unquenched, unchecked, unsatiated.

Rapturous hot kisses of passionate desire,
Extended stimulating massage-stroking hugs,
That exhilaration of flesh, sensually-inspired,
Lovemaking has just commenced and begun.

The genuinely supreme gratification
For the individual majority of most all of us

Is the explosive fireworks of sexual orgasm,
A grand titillation, a fabulous phantasm,
The apex of all of our craving and lust.

I find that what is so much more satisfying,
A rush that is overwhelming and totally euphoric,
What is especially much more gratifying,
Is when one is very loved and faithfully adored.

THE BALLAD OF
THE SHIPWRECK EL FARO
(LA BALADA DE EL NAUFRAGIO, EL FARO)

She was previously known as the Northern Lights,
Sea Star Line's Ship Of Tomorrow;
With rolling freight and large-containerized cargo,
She was later rechristened the El Faro.

Sailing from Jacksonville, Florida to Puerto Rico,
Drastic weather changes were quite unforeseen;
Tragically, on October 2nd, 2015,
She crashed into the horrific Hurricane Joachim.

Surging waves had risen to 50 feet high.
Battered by high winds and rough seas,
Desperate transmissions were being sent from the ship,
"Mayday! Mayday!" the desperate Captain pleads.

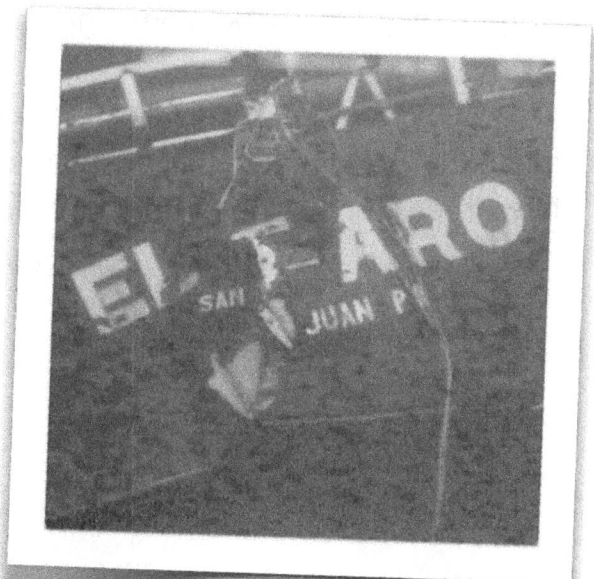

The Captain proclaimed he had lost all propulsion,
No time left from which to borrow.
The sea was a wild and frothy emulsion,
Such a dreadful, somber tale of sorrow.

The crew disembarked in their emergency rafts,
The ship was listing, rolling and reeling;
Innocent victims of the infamous Devil's Triangle,
Sailors gripped by a frenzied, desperate feeling.

The ship had been found in an upright position,
The U.S. Navy has recently discovered;
It had gone to the bottom in one single piece,
None, no survivors were ever recovered.

There are no more rays shining upon the El Faro,
This headlamp, this beacon of light;
Seven hundred and ninety feet full of cargo,
Sailing through the dark, stormy night.

It was here today, suddenly gone tomorrow,
Fifteen thousand feet to this deepwater keep.
Thirty-three went to the bottom of the sea,
To Davy Jones' Locker, submerged very deep!

THE JOY OF THE BIRTHDAY BOY

Ricky Boy, he's cute, he's the lucky one;
From the girls, he had better learn to run!
Oh, how fun it is, when you turn 21,
The world is your oyster, you lucky Son of a Gun!

When desirable women are thinking
For them, that you are the only one,
Stay humble, stay caring, my Son;
It's your choice, you can pluck any plum.

Stick to your compass degree.
It is true you will become,
Whomever you wish to be.
Steer clear of bad fortune,
And you will see.

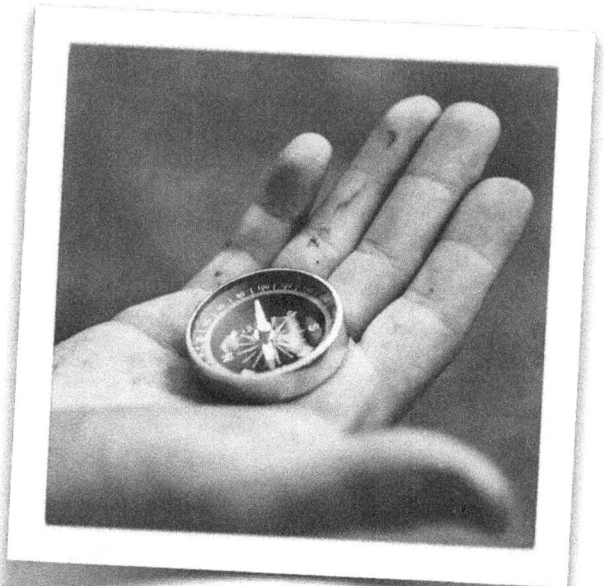

Map out the road, do not have any fear,
It is up to your focus, do not waver or veer.
The Natural Laws of Attraction
Will deliver all you hold dear.

Visualize your life, your job,
Your house, your gorgeous Wife,
Your beautiful Children,
Without any personal strife.
All good things that you desire
Eventually they are bound to appear.

So with a clink of our beers,
I toast you: "Be of good cheer,
For you this will be, a Very Good Year!"

THINGS THAT GO BUMP IN THE NIGHT

There are lots of folks, who think that ghosts,
Are nothing more than a hoax;
But let me exhort you, entreat you,
Admonish and beseech you!
Seriously, the fact is that this isn't a joke.

Banging, slamming windows and doors,
Bewailing, pandemonium,
Infiltrating, iniquitous discord.
Distinct and diversified,
Loud eerie noises,
Echoed distant cries.

Spirits and multi-colored orbs,
Passing right through your torso,
Instantly chilling one's body cold;
Like walking into a freezer locker.
Do not be brave, do not be bold.

Get out of that house
Before an evil presence
Starts to take over
Your spiritual essence!

Of your soul, it will attempt to grasp and choke,
Of your substance, it tries to clasp and hold.
Should I reiterate what you were just told?

A Poltergeist can follow you anywhere,
So take care, do not linger, do not stare.
In that space, as soon as you become aware,
You better be scared, quickly pack your things,
And rapidly, get the Hell out of there!

Do not dally, do not dare to compare,
Or have an adorable, ghost-hunting affair,
With whomever these entities might be.
Because we live in 3D, and we cannot see,
Where, or what places, or other dimensions
That they may originate from, full of dissension.

Extricate yourself from that place!
Run, do not act foolish and dumb!
Before it adheres and attaches its face,
To the hair on the back of your bum!

WITH ABUSION COMES CONFUSION
PART I

In the month of June in 1968,
We did a repeat of our last year's Spring Break.
Bubba's Uncle Barney sent us some mail;
He had four jobs waiting for us,
Detailing new and used cars,
Way down south, in Ft. Lauderdale.

Again we jumped into Bubba's camper truck,
And off we went, with just a few bucks.
In total years, we were just young teens,
I was sixteen, they were seventeen.
We were outwardly cocky,
And exceedingly naive and green.

First of all, we had to stop by and make a call,
To Bubba's Dear Old Grandma,
Who was forced into marriage at thirteen;
Said she divorced the bastard at fifteen.

She wanted us to stop
In little Piggott, Arkansas,
To stop and see her kin,
Where she had lived
Way long before
She had moved to Michigan.
Since it was Bubba's camper truck,
We did not have any luck;

We were woefully insufficient,
Getting him to alter his decision.
Attempts at dissuading him
Were fruitless, not very convincing;
To abort, to just drop his pursuit,
Of this personal, family mission.

Then we planned to travel on,
To our next destination, expeditiously.
Down to bug-infested Marx, Mississippi,
To visit yet another family clan,
Where there were so many more of them.

After suffering a Bedbug Trauma,
All over our legs and our feet,
We headed on towards Alabama,
Looking for some wide-open concrete.

After finding the Interstate Highway,
We made a pit stop delay;
It was a lonely service station,
And it included an all-night cafe.

Anticipating a cup of black coffee,
A clean windshield and a full tank of gas,
Enough juice to get us on through
This fading, old Confederate Nation,
Wasting away, these low-wage paying,
Antiquated, old cotton plantations.

Bubba got his coffee,
For only 15 cents;
Meanwhile, standing outside,
I was gassing up the tank.

He said that the Law Dawg inside
Had the waitress up close,
Really absorbing his mind.
It was a bad time that I chose,
When I decided to ask her why,
She had charged me 25 cents;
It was one whole extra dime.
The Sheriff reached for his gun,
And in a low voice he growled,
"You better leave swiftly now, Son,
And I think you had better run!"

When I told Bubba what had happened,
And that she had charged me 25 cents,
Laughing, he said "You dumb Yankee Boy,
You'd better start practicing
Your Redneck Southern accent!"

Teddy, Sam and Bubba all slept in the back;
They were always conniving
For me to do all of the driving.
I stayed on the highway, heading east;
I was not at all sleepy, in the least.

The 8-Track stereo was jamming
With Roger Miller and Johnny Rivers;

They were just a'singing and palavering;
Just about then, I really got the shivers.
Abruptly a brilliant, blazing bright light,
And then suddenly, instantly for me,
It was "Baby Good Night!"
And I went completely out like a light.

The next thing I remember,
I was driving down a dark, lonely road;
A heavy fog was clouding my brain,
In a trance, I was just driving my load.

Nowhere could I find a highway sign,
But lo, and behold, I found
Two GIs thumbing a ride.
On the side of the road,
Amidst multitudes of giant, bug-eating toads,
Sat two lonely, uniformed Army guys.
That was all, in the swamp, in the dark,
In the middle of nowhere, that I was able to find.
They sat under a streetlight, not a car in sight,
Soaking up raindrops, hopefully bumming a ride.

Interestingly enough,
The croakers on the highway
Like pancakes were flattened.
Their entrails distended,
All squished and compressed;
An amphibious bloodbath,
A road-dampened mess.

I asked "How far east would you boys be a-going?"
They said "We are not heading east, my friend.
We are heading down south to New Orleans,
And so are you, or haven't you seen?"
I said "No, I seem to be missing something,
Clearly I must have been sleep-driving,
Or possibly I maybe was drive-dreaming.
It seems I'm about three hours away,
From any recent, conscious memory."

We rode on together,
Till we came to a junction,
Where they could head south,
And I could turn left, driving east,
In a fog, attempting to still function.

My mind seemed to skip,
For the rest of the trip.
My faculties seemed feathery,
A confused, befuddled memory;
It never completely lifted its veil.
I was dazed and perplexed,
Until we finally reached Ft. Lauderdale.

I had never done drugs, only tried a few beers,
Very emotionally-stable, I lived without fear.
You may scoff at me now, or you may not believe,
But *you* too may be missing, some of your memory;
Memory gone missing, that you may never retrieve!

WITH ABUSION COMES CONFUSION
PART II

Back in 1968,
I drove to the Irish Hills racetrack,
But I got there, only to find
The event had been canceled.
I called up my parents and explained that
I wasn't ready to go back.
So instead of returning back home,
I wanted to go to a Chicago museum,
To look at some dinosaur bones;
They said "That's all right," they condoned.

Driving up the side of Lake Michigan,
Three times I was stopped,
Searched me for weapons,
Patted down by the Cops.

I rolled out my sleeping bag,
On a Catholic Church lawn,
Just to catch a few winks,
Get some sleep before dawn;
But someone inside,
Kept flicking the lights off and on,
So before the Cops came,
It was better to keep moving on.

I left North Chicago very late,
It was the weekend of the Presidential

Democratic convention
Of the notorious Chicago Eight.

I was then just an innocent,
Almost-seventeen-year-old lad.
Three times by the Police,
I had been personally harassed.
I was now leaving town,
Most incredibly mad.

My trusty Iron Horse,
Was a Triumph 650, of course.
I was run out of town,
By a Fascist Police Force.

I had had no idea of the seriousness
Of the young Yippie Movement and its new anarchists

Coming to the National Democratic Convention;
And just because of my adolescent young age,
During stop-searches,
Cops threatened me with Juvenile Detention!

Mayor Daly had just recently issued to the Police
Billy Clubs, Riot Helmets, Mace, new riot techniques;
Barbed-wire checkpoints, like Military installations,
Also the latest in Armed Forces Communications.
Just in case things should become difficult or hard,
He was backing it up with the National Guard!

Driving through South Chicago at 2 AM,
The bars emptied out Brothers,
Again and again.

Whiskey and wine bottles,
Were flying roundabout my head.
I was steering and veering,
I thought I might end up dead.

I was doing about 90 miles an hour,
There was little or no traffic,
So I gave it more Power.
Even if the lights turned crimson red,
I just kept going full tilt,
Full speed straight instead!

I blasted through Gary, Indiana;
It was a lot more of the same.
To get to the Highway,

It wasn't a kid's game.

Across the Michigan border I flew;
I was making great time,
And I thought I'd be home soon.

Suddenly, I was quite overwhelmed,
By a super-bright, white light,
Then instantly, once again,
It was sleep tight, "Baby Good Night!"

When my brain woke up again,
I was on a lonely, dark country road,
The pea-soupy fog was so dense,
Although the air was incredibly cold.

Forty miles an hour, no lights, and no signs,
What happened? Nothing seemed to make sense.
But with the North Star guiding me,
I rightly assumed, my direction from whence.

I made a U-turn,
But I could not, for sure ascertain,
If I had been transplanted,
Or if I had even been detained.

To find the eastbound highway,
By heading due south,
I saw a bright light in the morning dawn,
It was a Commercial Bank of some kind,
Off of the highway, all alone in the fog.

I rode up to the front door,
Just to look at their clock,
When I was suddenly hit,
With quite a bit of a shock—
It was half past six o'clock!

Three hours of time were missing,
But I still had most of my gas in the tank.
As I attempted to ponder this,
I was feeling so bewildered—
What was it that I had missed?

Guess who shows up,
But a cruiser, of small-town Cops;
My abusion, and my confusion,
It just didn't seem to stop.

I waved and took off,
And as the sun started coming up,
I found the Highway forthwith,
Lickety-split,
And I made it home soon,
By that late afternoon.

I said "HI" to the folks, and went directly to bed,
I slept sixteen hours, no kidding, no joke!
Happily on Sunday, my seventeenth birthday,
August 29th, from a deep sleep I finally awoke.

Opinion

A ROOKIE POET EXPOUNDING INTROSPECTIVELY*

Art needs freedom, to be more inventive,
Visuals restrained, bland, too normative,
Trapped in one genre, too stale, dormitive,
Writing from within, rapture elative,
Personal moments, caring, amative,
Unusual tales are provocative,
Mimicking authors, those emulative,
Engaging romance, ardent, emotive,
Passions unfurled, shamelessly effusive,
Inspiration with purpose yet to give.

A Century Poem - ten lines with ten beats each

FIRST IN THE VERSE

I find Carl Sandburg
Somewhat weird, and a wee bit confused.
Occasionally Robert Frost
Can be a little obtuse.
I would personally choose
My most beloved poet of all,
The one that is, certainly,
The most familiar to all.
The one with the most talent and skills,
The optimum literary juice;
My Personal Favorite—
The sophisticated Dr. Seuss!

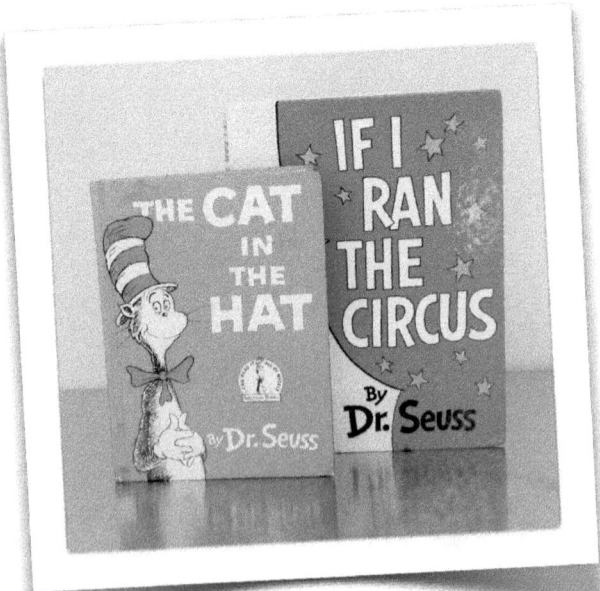

GMOs HAVE GOT TO GO!

When we put cross-species genes into our food,
It absolutely does not do any of us any good.
Your bodies were not made for genetic abuse,
Use the brain you were given, to pick well and choose!
Genes that are added to plants, from salmon and sheep,
Put your body in shock, makes it difficult to sleep.

'Groundup' is an herbicide,
That is incredibly, intensively deadly.
It is introduced to the plants
In a very-fatal cocktail-medley.
The seeds are soaked in insecticide poison,
Chemicals so very toxic, most incredibly.
If it can kill weeds, beetles and bugs,
It may kill you efficiently, most impeccably.
Your children could be irreparably altered,
Descendants may be deformed permanently,
Like cancer-filled mice in the laboratory.

We sell garbage to children,
From vending machines in the school.
Low-budget, cheap-quality cafeteria food,
A protein-replacement called Pink Drool.
Even those sweet sugar molecules,
In most beverages are abused.
So many bad choices (less value than dog food),
From which to choose.

If people were smart,
Metal lunch boxes would once again be cool,
And for disguising contraband,
Brown lunch bags always used to rule.

We love plausible denial and disbelieving,
We refuse to believe, what we are seeing.
GMOs are so incredibly bad
That even disorganized Europe has banned.
Europe only buys Archer Daniels Midland
(Called ADM for short),
They don't use those American GMOs,
That make Americans look so engorged.

Using GMOs, filling us full of soybeans and corn,
Foods that are known to make baby mice abort.
Corporate fake news media
In cahoots, still continues to distort.

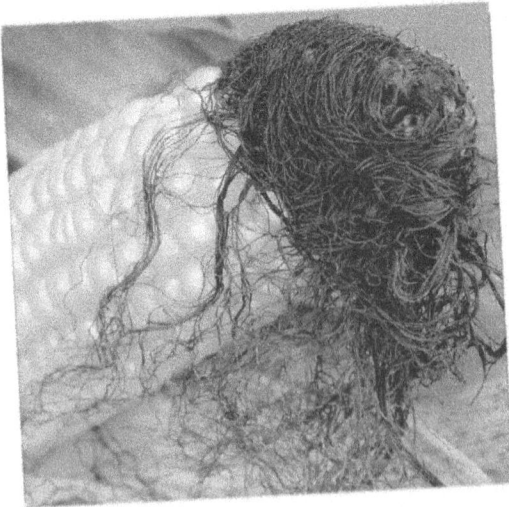

Even the starving masses
In North Korea have banned them;
They do not want them,
Whether we've frozen or canned them!

If we keep getting our groceries
From 'Con-Kill-Ya' and 'Dead-Tonto,'
Our future generations
Are already as dead as Geronimo!

Powerful enough,
To make even wharf rats become impotent,
After three generations,
Our sperm will be unproductive, immobile.

MR. FUNNY GUY'S ATROCITIES

The free-spirited 1960s,
They were magical, wonderful times;
We had so much naive optimism,
Best of all, there was very little crime.

With Kennedy, the Peace Corps, and God's good grace
We were still far ahead, in the Nuclear Race.
Rocket ships were shooting, off into space
America was then such a marvelous place!
Modern wonders, Saturday night drag car races,
Left us with optimistic, bright, beaming faces.

We had antibiotics and polio shots,
Smallpox and tuberculosis vaccinations,
Summertime National Park vacations,
With our friends and our family relations.

Modern wonders like color TV and transistor radios,
Reel-to-reel tape recorders and Hi-Fi stereos.
Drive-In hamburger stands and Roller Derbys,
Go-kart racing and also Demolition Derbys.
Being cool, and hanging out at the hamburger stands,
Meeting girls from other schools, dancing to new bands.

DC comic books were cheap entertainment
For only a dime,
Superman, The Flash, Green Lantern,
Batman, Cat Woman,

Green Arrow, Aqua Man,
Atom, and Wonder Woman;
Fantasy escapes for kids,
From the urban to the suburban.

Comedians for television
Who were way too risqué,
Some that had too-sexy,
Or vulgar repartee,
Those stand-up comics began
To record 33 rpms;
It was the only place that they could talk
About Carnal Sin!

But the J-E-L-L-O Pudding Man,
Trusted by everyone during his prime,
Was secretly the most-scandalous,
Despicable pillager of his time;

Highly respected, a moral comic, a mime.
Unbeknownst to entirely almost everyone,
He was committing big-time heinous crime!
The most utmost, reprehensible, evil beast,
That was ever created out of alluvial slime.
Only recently revealed, to be a Reviled Rapist,
Who committed his crime, more than 49 times!

He was the funniest (tied with Carlin for first place);
Using Quaaludes, such beautiful women he disgraced.
A Serial Rapist, such a contemptible criminal case,
Surreptitiously he managed to leave not a trace.
He was not a moral, not a stand-up guy for his race.

Such evil that he had created by design,
Playing a loyal sidekick, a straight-up good guy;
We watched him each and every week in Prime Time,
On the television show that was called "I Spy."
As a TV Father, he was always beaming and smiling,
And rolling his big, brown, very-trustworthy eyes;
He really liked to pontificate and moralize.

Later accused of abusing young women
That he had unscrupulously familiarized;
The local star-struck Hollywood authorities
Just kept ignoring those women's desperate cries.

A new comedy routine, not a favorite of mine,
That he later released, in a more recent time,
A skit about washing your ass;
It was so very weird, and very crass.
106

He was so very disgusting;
He did not have any class.

It seemed so venal, sordid and crude,
Suddenly he was shamefully rude.
Frustrated that some of his drugged victims
Did not always have squeaky-clean behinds!
His passionate public hygiene plea,
On his long-playing record of comedy,
Fantasizing in his twisted, squirrelly mind,
Was how he had maniacally hoped
To further enable his dastardly crimes.
He expected his female quarries
To always be cleansed and sanitary,
In case of possible pillage and rape.

This pig with the bland, homely face,
Had become such a disgusting disgrace.
What a twisted mind,
Committing his crimes,
Pulled down from his pedestal,
Just like Stalin and Hussein.

A Poster Boy for Television Seasons,
While women were having nightmares,
Awaking from their sleep, screaming.
This is how we will always remember
This despicable and loathsome,
Vile, degenerate, pretender!

OSTRICHES

Why do the Ostriches
Keep putting their heads in the sand?
Could it be just *because they can*?

Trying to hide their personal fears,
About their global warming jitters.
Determined and utterly resolved never to hear,
That destructive weather patterns are about to appear.
The facts that they ignore most indubitably,
Uppermost, wishing to avoid most absolutely,
But about which they are privately agitated,
Eating Vegan and blaming cows that flagellated.

Because of the free money
That exudes from the ground,
All filthy and dirty,
Wherever Oil is to be found;
Direct from the Devil,
That profusely abounds.

Unfairly it comes down to only a select few
Egocentrically hoarding all of the wealth,
But the Devil is determined to get his full due,
For sacrificing the Planet's Future Health.
The unquenchable need,
All of the insatiable greed,
Defying the baleful, blackened sky;
The burning, tearful, bloodshot eyes.

Putrid, acidic, fouled poisonous air,
Corporate investors will always declare
They are not empathetic, they really don't care.
They are not liable, not in the least culpable,
Staying self-indulgent, protected, unanswerable.

That gray malignant all-smothering smog,
Surrounding so thickly, one can't even jog!
Illimitably spreading asthma and cancer,
Efficiently permeating faster and faster.
Omnisciently it so pervasively abounds,
In most of the children all around.
Everywhere across this vast country,
It creates so much strife,
And it shortens the life,
Of all living things,
Wherever life can be found.

No matter how much the aloof Ostriches
Lying and denying, remaining oblivious,
There will be no prospective rebirth
For our dearly beloved Mother Earth!

PLEASE PEACE, PLEASE PEACE, PLEASE!

In these times of insufficient
Facilities for basic human needs,
In these times of exorbitant
And abundant personal greed,
All of these prophetic warnings
That we do not pay any heed,
And all of those starving children
That we ignore and do not feed.

We support the Secret Government,
And subsidize corporate travel in space.
Apparently we have overhead, above us
And also underground, undisclosed alien races.
Our fears are that they want to take over control
So we have to keep them hidden in secret places.
We now have many exclusive medical cures
But only for the super-rich, the financially pure!

Whistleblowers have been telling us
The Secret Government has gone Satanic.
That the exceptionally evil Beelzebub
Is still trying to take over the Planet.
And if you try and out the Guy,
You are branded a religious fanatic.

They tell us that a global government
Will make us all happily ecstatic.
No longer is it about our society,

Our humanity, and the public good,
As they poison our water
And feed us Frankenstein food.
Freely burn all of our oxygen,
And cut down what is left of our wood.
We know that we can do much better,
And we know that we unquestionably should!

What can we do?
Is there hope?
What is our fate?
Think positive thoughts,
Perform prayer and meditate?
Be a non-conformist,
A dissenter, a heretic, an apostate?

If you don't agree with the premise,
Limit how much you participate.
Soon we must get together
Or I estimate,
Before long there will be
Nothing left to postulate!

POLITICAL INCORRECTNESS

Have you noticed the Gays
That act like 'Gunderson Blooper,'
Intentionally reminding us
Of his cute little pooper?
Silver spoon in his mouth,
Riding on his shining white horse,
With a pink rose on his shoulder,
Saying,"Have you no remorse?"

The Feminists, the Lesbians,
The NAACP in the news,
Both sides of the Cubans,
With their opposite political-views.

The Puerto Ricans, the Mexicans,
Central Americans too,
Especially don't forget
Those welfare-case Russian Jews.

The Chinese and the Koreans,
Don't forget the Southeast Asians too;
Their various disparate claims,
It makes me uptight and confused.

Evangelists, Catholics, Mormons,
Protestants and Masons too,
The Muslims and Wiccans,
All of their diverse religious views.

The Handicapped, the Mentally Retarded,
The Emotionally Disturbed;
Everyone wants special attention,
It leaves me somewhat unnerved.

Aryans, Cartels, Crips and Bloods,
All get me quite perturbed;
Overwhelmed, quite annoyed,
Jaded, emotionally inured.

The Tweakers, the Junkies,
And all of those creepy-crawly Dregs,
The thieves and the gangsters,
Runny-nosed, frozen Cokeheads.

All of the neighborhood-corner dealers,
Trying to earn some street Cred;
This humongous bunch of losers,
Would be much better off dead.

The Terrorists, the Anti-terrorists,
The Police and the Feds,
Corporate polluters, sex traffickers,
Poached animals, all bled.

I'm sick of the whining and lying
And all of the insolent pretentiousness,
The obnoxious, outrageous behavior,
And all of the annoying contentiousness.

Quit your snivelling and your crying,
Your constant bullshit and your lying;
Go out and gang up on your bullies,
Quit looking to everyone for free goodies!
You fat blinky Twinkies quit sighing,
You limp skinny wimps, stop your whining.

Every time someone offends you,
You get your panties in a bunch;
Toughen up and build some muscle,
Before you get handed your lunch!

POLLUTION

We all so desperately need resolution,
Imperative that we create a solution,
To save the Earth from our own destruction,
Our feculent, foul, filthiness and pollution.

Capitalism is a philosophy,
Of abject fatalistic suicide.
All of our '-isms' have failed us;
The absoluteness is no longer denied.

The only cure for Gaia's ills
Has become Total Global Genocide.
As far as following the Laws of God,
Only half of us try to apply and abide;
It makes the health of the planet plunge,
Into a dark, destructive, Ecological Slide.

It is an increasingly-accelerated, hypersonic slide,
A present-day, roller-coaster, amusement park ride.
To depend on eclipsing unrestricted growth,
And human post-haste, out-paced overpopulation,
This plan is a very substandard business model,
If we expect to have any future generations.

Corporations that often continually
Keep on spreading outward militarily,
Proliferating freely like an infectious disease.
An unquenchable need for greed, unappeased,

Unlimited power, thievery, rapacity,
Insatiable proclivity for avidity.

In the animal kingdom,
There is a truth we must face,
That it is only our race that has
Become galactically renowned.
For what we have done to this place
We should be ashamed of ourselves;
It is a tragic, species-related disgrace!

STOCK MARKET CHARTS

When you want to buy stock,
You don't want to be shocked,
You don't want to get clocked,
You don't want to get socked.

Or your portfolio to get thoroughly trashed,
Having your money get hashed very fast.
Sliding prices are taking a lot of your cash;
Poor investments have taken half of your stash.

Don't want to take a bath,
You must do all the math.
Taken, completely soaked,
Your money goes up in smoke.

Hear my fast-beating heart,
Where the Hell do I start?
Stock Market shopping cart,
Or should I buy on a lark?"

I could give you stock tips,
From the side of my lips.
Best-dividend Blue Chips!
Emerging Market picks!

Instead, I would rather share,
Only because I care,
And I wish to impart,

To give you a fresh start.
What is simple indeed,
This is just what you need,
To learn how to read,
Any Stock Market feeds.

There are only three things,
The Market can possibly bring;
Three very simple things,
For your clear understanding.

Zigzagging upwardly,
Zigzagging downwardly,
It keeps trying to reach;
Climbs on back to its apex.
Two or three attempts to reach,
To extend the zenith at its peak.
Stocks will not continue to seek,
When the momentum is too weak.
To break on through to the peak,
That is when the Market begins
To start reversing its trend.

That is when you quick sell,
As most rapidly as you can.
Or your savings will begin to wend,
On their way back down again.
The chart-line will zigzag on down,
Until it reaches its deepest valley.
It will vie, two or three tries.
When it fails to go deeper,

That is when you put up your money and buy;
That is when you watch your money go Sky High!

(For the third possibility,
I have a lot of hostility,
For you cannot jiggle your way out
Of The Sideways Wiggle.)
This third trend, most importantly,
When it goes sideways consistently,
Do not laugh and do not giggle,
Do not bother to bicker or quibble,
Because the Market can jiggle,
For a very long time, in a Sideways Wiggle.

That is when you stay away,
There is no way
To tell which way,

How you should make your play.

You cannot be foretold,
When it will break away;
It could be today,
Or maybe many months away.

If it breaks out to the upside,
Give it a ride.
If it trends down,
Wait till it hits the ground;
Lots of bargains can soon be found.

I do not intend to be flippant,
But I wish not to skip it;
What's popularly known to all as the Santa Claus Rally.
Every year you can plan to tally
A whole lot of money consistently,
On the annual return of the Santa Claus Rally.

It has yielded positive returns
In 34 of the past 44 holiday seasons;
The last five trading days of the year,
And the first two trading days after New Year's.
It is almost 78% guaranteed;
Even you can make,
A lot of money, indeed!

Sadly, the Christmas of 2015
Was a weak Christmas season;
Another repeat of 1999.

But the Christmas of 2007,
Was the worst Santa Claus Rally
That I have ever seen!
It ushered in the Crash of 2008,
The second-worst Bear Market
Since the Crash in 1929 rampaged.

2016, at this moment, has been very lean;
It is looking pretty harsh, pretty mean!
It has been a yearlong Sideways Wiggle,
It was almost impossible to make a nickel!

TEN SUBLIMINAL TV MESSAGES THAT TARGET WOMEN

Conveyed with illusory advertising,
While they are indoctrinating and proselytizing,
With deceptive and manipulative script writing,
Hollywood with its Agenda, is deviously seducing.
Producers deleteriously producing,
Always disingenuously deluding.
Here are ten examples describing,
Their personally-biased point of view.
These samples here, are just but a few:

1 Men are so stupid and dumb,
How easily they will succumb,
To all of their sexual desires;
You will easily light them on fire,
While their brains become
Thick-witted and numb.

2 About you, they don't have a clue,
They have no idea what is new.
They are not really aware,
They do not care what they wear,
While they are publicly embarrassing you.

3 There is no need to go to school,
It is easy to find you a fool.
Just be a pretty and sexy young lady,
Till he gives you a ring or a baby,
It is easy to find you a tool.

4 Do not cook, he must be trim;
Do not clean, it's up to him.
You have girlfriends and dancing,
Lots of primping and prancing,
He will pay your dues at the gym.

5 They still keep thinking
They can wear socks with their sandals,
That they can wear black socks with shorts;
Their fashion IQ is a mission abort.

6 And all of their favorite History Channels,
And all of the Business Station Reports;
Those are the only entertainment decisions,
That they will watch on their boring television.

7 Those are the only shows
That men are willing to watch;
And they dress like a GQ Sasquatch.
Too lazy to shave, and they usually stink,
Improbable that these morons
Can still manage a thought left to think.

8 Ineffectually unable of showing sympathy,
Nothing but beer-drinking mediocrity.
Incapable of having a Night Show personality,
Men must be trained for minimal sensitivity.

9 Learning not to miss
While they are taking a piss.
Always begging us for our forgiveness,

For who knows whatever is next,
Always worshiping their own manliness.
TV has become a female fantasy,
While marriage is the major casualty.
A pretend world lacking all reality.
Misguiding all the women's dreams,
Teaching dirty tricks and vile schemes.

10 It is no longer necessary to have the will
To build up lasting relationship skills;
If you don't always get what you want,
Just pout like a petulant dilettante.
Then sit down and watch Dr. Phil,
Have a drink, and pop another pill.

UNDYNAMIC DUO

About the infamous 'Dental Pest' and 'Craze E,'
It appears there is nothing really there to see.
Inventing a pretense of acting gallant,
But sorely lacking any musical talent.

Attempting to be some bad-ass Gangsta Heroes,
These are two of Entertainment's Biggest Zeros.
As to their own musical so-called "artistry,"
Such a lack of talent, is amazing to me.

Their performances are so incredibly boring;
Bragging about Booty Calls, and nympho-male whoring.
'Craze E' seems to be some sort of Financial Wizard;
'Dental Pest' is more like a Nonsensical Lizard.

No self-reproach, about being "kept" men;
Nothing but Hollywood Courtesans.
They are inefficacious and impuissant,
Foo-Foo dogs; two children subservient.

And what is even more humiliating than that?
'Dental Pest's' 'Big Buns Bunny Honey'
Is out there spending quintillions and gazillions,
But she won't give any more money to that Big Dummy!

'Dental Pest' was caught shamelessly publicly begging
Facebook's young CEO for fifty-two million!
Now do you want to hear a sick story about Bling?

'Craze E' once shot his brother, just for taking his ring!
If not for his connection to 'Dedunce,'
'Craze E' would today be a Nobody!

But the real tragedy, financially, I am afraid,
Is that their main source of revenue
Comes from the poor, Inner City kids,
Who are already suffering economically
In their neighborhoods on the Skids.

Poetry Forms

HAIKU

1 Love will procreate,
Friendship will cohabitate,
Lust will dominate.

2 Memories sparkle,
Like bright, glistening dewdrops,
On the uncut grass.

3 Cano is so smooth,
He gets the team in the groove,
And we added Cruz!

4 Mother, I love you,
For all that you've done for me,
Creating me free.

LIMERICKS

1 There once was this cute girl named Tammy,
Who came all the way from Miami.
She loved to tan in the sun,
Showing her cute little buns,
Her dives in the pool were dynamic!

2 I once dated a girl from New York;
So fine, I was afraid of the Stork.
Regularly down on my knees,
Eternally begging her "Please,"
Marriage was my last resort!

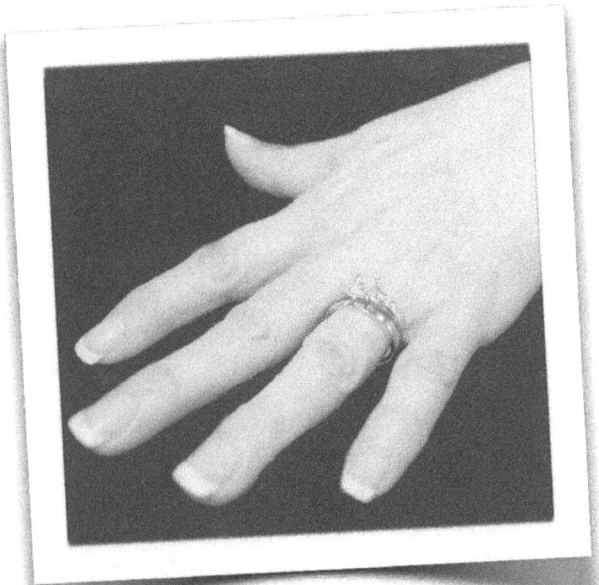

3 I once met a girl that was Amish,
I said she could make me a promise.
She swore she would never tell,
If I lovingly rang her bell,
Enjoyably, mission was accomplished!

4 I once met a cute girl from Nashville,
She was very sweet but so bashful,
I said, "You are my kind of girl,
I have just found my precious pearl!"
She said, "You are one nervy rascal!"

5 I once romanced a girl from Seattle,
To date her was a bit of a battle;
For so many weeks I did flirt,
Until she let me under her skirt,
And made me promise never to tattle!

6 Let the hucksters try to practice a little more decorum.
Improprieties keeping their togas on at the Forum.
The Public desperately repetitious to implore them,
While the Politicians disingenuously adore them,
Doublespeak always reigning incessantly, ad nauseam.

QUOTES

1 Beware of anyone
who tries to convince you
that your opinion is important.
They are only trying
to make you look foolish,
or attempting to take your money, or both.

2 Nothing will shorten your life
more expeditiously
than borrowing money.
And all the more so,
if you use less-than-legitimate sources.

3 The only thing Congress knows how to run
is a golf cart.

4 Nothing ever changes but the psychology.

5 Seventy-five percent of nuthin' is nuthin'.
Fifty-percent of sumpthin' is sumpthin'!

6 If you wish to be a writer,
you must ignore the naysayers,
and write at least two hours every day.

7 I find that it is much easier to write well
than it is to speak well,
and much easier to pre-empt my mistakes!

8 If you give up your guns,
the savages will take over!

9 A poem is like a child -
once you create it,
it never leaves you.

10 We used to wear clothes
that were handmade to fit us,
now we try to wear clothes
that are best fitted for machines.

11 Life is too short to be wasting time
watching commercials!

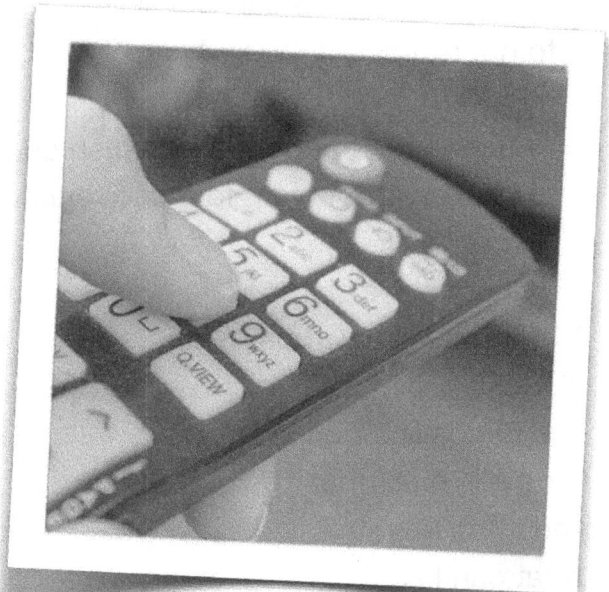

12 From my personal observations,
it seems very likely to me,
that those that are doing
the lion's share of protesting about high taxes
are highly likely to be the same people
that are cheating or defrauding
the utmost on their own taxes.
And subconsciously they think
it is a good strategy,
to attempt to sway public opinion,
just in case they are caught, captured, seized,
or put under Federal arrest;
investigated, exposed, disclosed, discovered, unveiled,
unsheltered, unsealed, unconcealed,
and publicly revealed, by the Feds.
That's about it!

13 The number one survival skill to master
Is to not run out of money!

14 My poems do not really flourish and shine
until I've rewritten them four or five times.

15 Chimps like chimps,
And wimps like wimps;
Gimps like gimps,
And pimps like pimps;
Blimps like blimps,
And imps like imps.
What can I say?

Birds with limp feathers,
Limp through life better together.

16 My Wife came with
a lot of excess personal baggage
when I married her,
and none of it
has left the garage
in the past 25 years!

SONNETS

1 M'LADY

Your downy touch is like a delicate, summer breeze.
Your scintillating smile, brings me down to my knees.
Your lovely voice, wherever, whenever heard,
Fills the air with the music of harmonic birds.
Smoldering eyes, liquid obsidian pools,
Glistening brightly, gleaming, sparkling jewels.
The pleasantly light, wafting caress of your breath,
Electrifies the small hairs, on the back of my neck.

Your tanned, kitten-soft, au naturel, smooth skin,
When fondled, feels silkier than soft, new satin.
That adorable dimple, that sits on your chin,
Gives you a most charming, most adorable grin.
To steal all of your heart, I'm pretty sure is a sin,
But to gain all of your love, is a Blue Ribbon Win!

2 M'LADY, I LOVE YOU

Her beauty is exquisite;
The Creator's own design.
Her temperament subdued,
Her disposition so sublime.
Her inclination is to always
Be so generous and kind;
A more magnificent woman,
This man is unable to find.

You may circle the world,
Always seeking that perfect girl,
Trying to get a glimpse,
Of that unique, unflawed pearl.
She is demure, not flirtatious, most attractively shy,
You cannot forget her, no matter how hard you try.

The covetousness, the fervor,
Just for a kiss,
To be in her presence,
Not a day I can miss.
My selfish, uncontrolled,
Unrestrained jealousness,
Just to hold her and to kiss her,
Is unbearable bliss.
Fascination and yearning,
An unrestrained eagerness,
A vision of beauty,
God's artistic inventiveness!

3 BIG JIM IN THE BIG 12*

Happy, dandy, randy, Michiganders,
Are those snappy, scrappy, strappy Wolverines.
Big Jim strategizes, he defies and defines,
Conventional football wisdom, its plays, new designs.

The Rubber Empire will not believe their eyes.
Those hayseeds we call The Ohio State Buckeyes,
They will soon realize, when they survey all around,
Determine, discover, that they have given up ground.

Uncovered, they have been reanalyzed,
Quartered, dismembered, dissected, resized.
Their Big 12 position, compromised, de-marginalized,
Because Big Jim's Offense, has been so well disguised.

Have you heard the new scuttlebutt,
That is going around?
Ann Arbor has a brand new,
Gun-slinging, Sheriff in town!

a Shakespearean-type Sonnet

4 LIFE IS UBIQUITOUS

Invisible presence is pervasive,
Celestial Creator, subtly persuasive.
Parallel universes, a discreet existence,
Humanity, just a fledgling adolescence.
A spiritual open door influence,
Experiencing our own existence,
A Fatherly omnipresence,
Enlarging and expanding your Sixth Sense.

Supreme Creator helping us maturate,
Shut down the media and meditate,
Wherefrom and wherefore contemplate,
It is a new paradigm to fascinate.
A transformative chrysalis,
A unique, special ontogenesis.

VILLANELLES

1 ROME FELL IN A DAY
Right now a lot of sad fans
Hanging around by the Bay,
Are not feeling too gay.

I say if they lose the game today,
They would forfeit their wild card pay;
There would be so very much dismay.

What a fray, a really bad day.
A mound of sound,
Measured in pounds.

Could be heard round and round,
The magnanimous Puget Sound,
Where old logging towns are found.

And the #12 clowns abound,
The Hawks rebound, confound, and astound,
Continue to pound Niners into the ground.

With repetition, the competition
Seems to have lost their volition.
They've given up their mission;
Been sent home to go fishing.

2 LOVE IS LIKE A BULLET TRAIN *

Love is like a Bullet Train,
Just like a hunter seeking prey;
A lonely man might have some game.

It starts with a fondness, turns to sweeping emotion,
A desire for friendship, with passions exploding;
A carnal lust, at the subtle caress of her clothing.

The understanding portrayed in her eyes,
The sparkling white gleam of her smile,
Is a neon display of her feminine wiles.

Creating feelings, protectiveness and benevolence,
Arousing thoughts of affectionate, flaming amorousness,
Cherished feelings of attachment, respectful tenderness.

The warmth of her touch, creates sentiments of fidelity,
An ardor of amour, bordering on worship and idolatry,
A heated fervor, relishing her feminine sexuality.

Sympathy, affection, and loving admiration,
Witnessing all of her adorable affectations,
Visual stimulations, turning into infatuation.
The train won't slow down, till it reaches its destination.

* (A Vanilla Villanelle)

3 FOR LIFE, WALKING UP

As the years, like the waves,
Keep roiling on up,
Transfixed on clouds in the heavens,
I keep looking up.
I have to keep pushing,
Moving straight forward on up.

Don't want my old creaky joints
To become all rusted up,
I have been watching my health,
And as the years add on up,
Getting closer to my Destiny,
But still not ready to give up.

Discipline, motivation,
I dial it on up,
Drinking and smoking,
It was a challenge giving them up,
I tell myself to keep pushing,
Moving straight forward on up.

Atrophy can set in, lack of movement,
From not turning it up,
Daily living becomes a challenge,
Of constantly shaping up,
Getting closer to my Destiny,
But still not ready to give up.

Good deeds are like pool balls,

Have to keep racking them up,
To be a good Father and Husband,
Always stepping it up,
I have to keep pushing,
Moving straight forward on up.

Still working on cleaning,
My personal resume up,
Before I get on God's elevator,
And start heading on up,
Getting closer to my Destiny,
But still not ready to give up,
I have to keep pushing,
Moving straight forward on up.

4 THE IMMUNITY OF A MARVELOUS COMMUNITY

Living among friends,
In a safe, secure community,
Enhances one's life,
And gives everyone more ability;
People united,
Creates a desirable reality!

The Parents
Legally armed and protected,
Family dogs
Quickly have intruders detected,
Scoundrels and sinners
Are quickly suspected.

Watchful, caring neighbors,
Gives one freedom with impunity.
A quality education,
Will blossom with diversity.
Cooperation with neighbors,
Gives us peace and tranquillity.

Potluck parties and barbecues,
With just a little beer and wine.
Sharing our home recipes,
And the latest clothing designs.
Safe, friendly neighborhood bars,
Therefore no need to drive.

Unfamiliar, new musical sounds

Freely abound.
Singing voices,
In schools and churches resound.
At Christmastime,
It is a lovely, glittering town.

Knowing sincere, sensitive neighbors,
That have genuine pity.
Happy voices from the youngsters,
Emanations clever and witty.
Squeals of joyful children thriving,
Playing in a delightful city.
A festive colony of joviality;
Friendly, domestic conviviality.

Politics

CLASSES OF THE MASSES

The Royalty loves to hear about loyalty
While they are boiling tea on the roiling sea.

The Bourgeoisie loves to see
People spending money most frivolously.

The Proletariat are the wariest.
Financially deleterious, but usually the merriest.

The Destitute have gotten the boot;
Having nothing left to lose, no other options to choose.

The Congress has digressed,
They have failed our requests.
They are an ignorant mess.

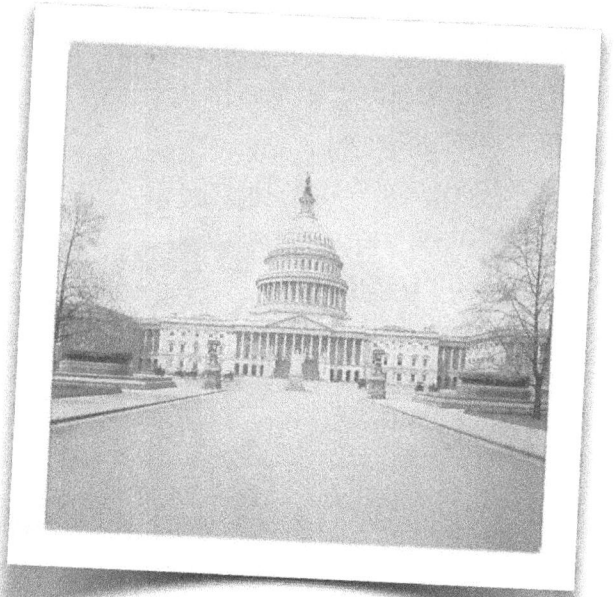

FIGHT, DON'T LOSE YOUR RIGHTS!

You are indebted to past generations,
Constitutional Rights, so purely precious and pleasing.
It is foolish to trade or negotiate away
Civil Immunity Protections for any reason.

Voracious politicians, pursuing positions of power,
Holding out carrots, always teasing.
Rapacious office seekers, who like to devour,
Crusading every campaign season.

Even though I fear the occasional madman,
A monster, who is cravenly making his plans;
Gunning down in public, our beautiful children,
Committing the most heinous, unforgivable sin!

Pathologically seeking redemption,
Murdering innocents,
When rampaging at the school,
Or the movieplex.
What they don't tell you,
Is that more than 80%
Have been *using*,
They're on long-term drug maintenance;
Addicted to Ritalin,
Ever since their pubescence.

Attention Deficit Hyperactivity Disorder Meds,
After ten years of a prescribed, Chemical dependence

They clearly are a bucket of worms,
A psychological mess.
But the Big Business of International, Corporate Pharma
Does not care very much,
How it creates dreadful Karma.

Villains have carefully selected their targets:
Unarmed, and exposed, defenseless, unguarded.
At a venue with innocents unprotected and at large,
With lax security, so easy to besiege and bombard.

Many of these evil, heinous attacks
Could have possibly been circumvented;
If teachers and mall security personnel
Were allowed to carry concealed weapons.

History will corroborate my hesitancy,
Because governments will seize as they please.
What is even more scary and dangerous
Is that of our rights, freedoms and liberties
How swiftly they can be taken away from us,
With a pen so easily outlawed and seized,
Erased from the public media and historical text
By our lackadaisical complacency
And the power of the elite, economically-entrenched.

Once you give up your rights,
They don't ever come back.
Just ask Hitler or Stalin
About their citizen attacks.
Always remember the words

Of the most-evil Mao Tse-Tung:
"Political power only comes
From the barrel of a gun."

Democracy always must have to be
A most-carefully guarded task.
It takes careful due diligence
To make it endure forever and last.
The publications of "Brave New World,"
And "1984" from the past
Should have already forewarned us,
Should have already taught us about that!

KOREAN DEMAGOGUE

This Korean dictator, 'Dim Dong-Moon,'
What a goon, what an iniquitous buffoon;
A Kimchi-Smelling, Pungent Personality,
What a frigging Humpty Dumpty cartoon!

He shoots his General, his Father's friend,
With a large anti-aircraft weapon!
So demonic and diabolically deranged;
Spread The General all over the firing range.

With a brain like an undeveloped Polliwog!
He went and fed his Uncle to hungry dogs!
A chubby and demented, Crazy Loon!
That wants to bring an end to the world very soon!

He ordered the public execution
Of his ex-girlfriend, Hyon Song-wol.
He is cruelly eliminating anyone,
Who might be a Threat To His Rule.

He accused her and half of her orchestra
Of performing pornography in China;
Anyone that he possibly might think,
Who could talk about his sexual privacy;
He accused her of orgies and debauchery,
Then he swiftly gave them all the Death Penalty.
Public executions
Are silencing the majority instead,

Now they are all dead;
His new wife wanted revenge.
No one even thinks of undermining him,
Or they disappear in a whirl.
One of the most foul, the cruelest of Dynasties,
In today's modern world!

An enigma,
A new modern Asian Caligula.
With satanic imaginations,
He has kinky fascinations,
Seeking demented titillations,
His existence is an abomination.

To all of humanity,
He is a giant Obelisk Of Insanity.
China's buffer zone could soon turn rogue,
Starting a nuclear war all alone,
By a madman sent, an emotionally disturbed tyrant,
With a fleet of nuclear drones,
Manifesting his emotional disease,
While threatening global peace;
Very soon we must purge
This vile, malevolent scourge!

'MR. MITTENS' MUFFED UP!

Mister Marshmallow,
Miscreant Man,
Morbidly Maligning,
Merrily Muckraking,
Menial Mudslinging,
Madly Moaning,
Morosely Murmuring,
Meretriciously Misleading,
Maliciously Mistreating,
Malevolently Marketing,
Masquerading Male,
Misguidedly Modulating,
Moribund Moronic Mormon!

PRESIDENTS

It doesn't really matter
If they are not cognizant,
Or verily regarded
As somewhat intelligent.

There is one constant, it seems,
Throughout these many years,
That all of the elected Presidents
Have very large satellite-dish ears.

THE BALLAD OF NAPOLEON

The name originates, it comes from Napoli,
It is now the expression "To be Napoleonic!"
The Emperor of Europe, he was predestined to be,
Until his selfish aspirations became demonic!

In public alone,
He did not wish to be seen,
Without his stunningly-lovely,
Darling sweet Josephine.
In public they had shown,
They liked to primp and to preen;
Of her eloquence and elegance,
He was exceptionally keen.

The Hapsburg Austrians,
The Prussians and the Russians,
Invaded and pillaged Paris, France.
Napoleon was apprehended this time;
Transferred and exiled, sent to Elba Island.
With the support of loyal friends he escaped,
An undertaking of another chance to liberate.

Finally he was defeated at Waterloo,
He surrendered and was captured by the British;
Banished to the small island of St. Helena,
Where confined, he became sadly diminished.
His multiple challenges just kept compounding,
Easily as many as hundreds of thousands;

He was responsible for a decade of death,
His reign caused so many to give up their last breath.

Maneuvering with his cannons in line,
He was brilliant, in his modern warfare design;
But his downfall was that luscious red wine,
Dishonorably-laced with poison, many times.

His anguish to all was most excruciating,
His condition was so terribly heartbreaking.
His rapid digression, was more than astounding,
Soldiers sacrificed, choices still are confounding.

TROUBADOUR

I did not verify, why should I?
I am the Jester, till the day I die!
I'll make you laugh, and I'll make you cry,
I will tell all the truths, and expose all the lies.

This morning I travel to new roads and new skies,
To remain a Free Man, to rebel and defy,
Unseal buried truths, injustices and crimes,
Reveal what has been, categorically denied,
About Kings and their Lords,
And their Government Spies.

Sports

BIG GAME HUNTING 2015

The Hawks are fighting back
With a new, five-pronged attack.
They got off to a slow start—
A broken-wheeled donkey cart;
They have now begun playing smart.
The QB has lately refound his hustle,
Using more of his intellectual muscle.
Fighting back to get the Wild Card,
The Receivers are doing what is hard;
Their numbers are off of the charts.

Our potent, tremendous, dynamic Defense,
Still has rapacious, voracious aggressiveness.
Humbly speaking it is my very best guess
(Please do not think I would carelessly jest)
Determination and teamwork always work best;
It is up to them if they pass this big test.

About our prestigious Legion of Boom,
Our cyclonic-whirlwind of deadly doom,
Using our special, heavy-duty industrial strength,
Will hydraulically crush your inefficient Offense;
The pressure has now become so incredibly intense.

Lately Spin Wizards and some pencil-necked Pundits,
Are fraught full of clichés, and lots of Whodunits?
Only three games left, to gain national prominence,
These mighty marauders of the Pacific Northwest,
Striking fear, fighting back, to be the Very Best!

DEFENSE

In the region of the rainy season
Roams the indomitable
Legion of Boom.

They like to groom
Their warriors so soon,
From cocoon to the plume,
From the womb to the tomb;
Into a powerful platoon
Of most fearsome Dragoons.

These big men do hale
From the land in the Dale,
Where many are pale,
Where brave Mariners do sail,
And soulful Killer Whales wail.

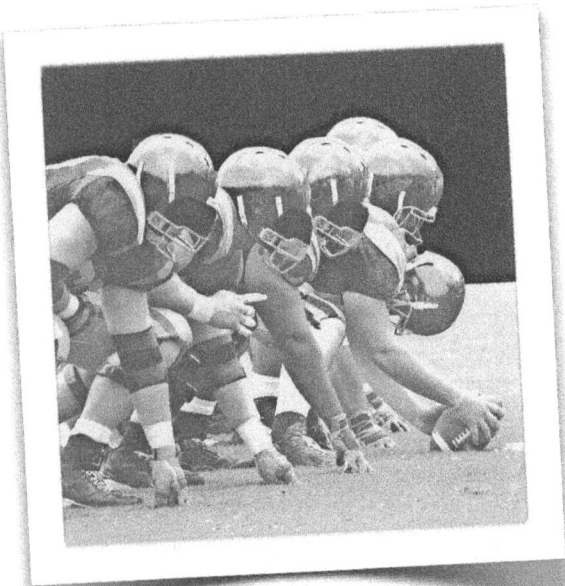

By the Washington Loch,
With the large, shipping docks,
With the thundering loud sonic booms,
Where the darkened foreboding clouds loom,
Streaked with white where the Thunderbirds zoom.

The mountains are clouded and shrouded with snow,
Where Bigfoot roams free, below glowing UFOs.
From out of the forest, and the ferns and the mist,
Comes a team so dismissed, and previously dissed;
They are seriously, so unquestionably pissed!

They have had so much time to fume,
This blue-streak lightning fast,
This brutal frightening cast,
This explosive TNT blast,
This audacious Legion of Boom.

They rain down in torrents;
No umbrella for you.
Quenched and drenched,
Hypothermic and blue.
There is nothing
That you can possibly do!
Gripped by the fear,
You run like the deer.
You steer and you veer.
Then quickly you skate.
Then you twist and rotate,
To avoid the big date

With the end of your fate.
But sadly for you, it is too late.
Just one skip with a slip,
You are enclosed in their grip.

With fear in your eyes,
With a whimper and a sigh,
You try not to cry.
For this is your last time,
It is your final goodbye,
It is your destiny dictated by,
This impassionate Legion of Boom,
Those intensely fierce Creatures of Doom!

DRAFT DAY

Are you starting to feel the rising excitement
Like the feeling you get from the Friday Night Fights?
Suppressing a squeal of anticipation,
To watch a new wave passing over the nation.

We controlled the ground at the Puget Sound,
And we pushed the load on the road.
And now having the truth be told,
Like bulldozers, onward they rolled.

And our anti-aircraft defense
Totally blanketed the skies;
Our chests were fully swelled with pride.
I will assume that there is no room,
Nowhere that the enemy can hide.
Last year when having tried, they died.
That was the price the enemy paid,
While sealing shut their own doom,
By the notorious and glorious,
The eminently-excellent, Legion of Boom.

There occurred one small flaw that we saw
At the end of the game, on the goal line this time,
And it stopped what was going to be called
The greatest of all comebacks,
Ever-before witnessed, in Superbowl Prime Times.

The wheels and the gears were turning
In General Manager John Schneider's mind.
And what super weapon did he find?
The greatest goal line pass threat around,
And he brought him back to the Puget Sound;
And unlike Tom Brady's Gronk,
This massive creature came
From the Black-And-Gold Swamp.

He moves like a high-speed NASCAR ghost,
And his arms are as big as a massive goal post.
So now Draft Day is the best time
To step up the Offensive Line,
To make strength and size the prize.

By drafting the lighting-quick,
Handsome and most-talented,
The nimble and swift Tyler Lockett,
We also added the need for speed,
To control the field and dominate.
That is what is in our Future,
That is what is on our Plate.

DYNASTY GONE
49ERS DEFROCKED AND DETHRONED!!

Out from the fold they were rolled,
And down to San Mateo they were sold.
Both the players and the fans, we are told,
Were discarded like dirt, unseen;
Just like removing mildew and mold,
Then spray-washed and dry-cleaned.

Big Jim could not be controlled,
The Brat wanted to scold.
The Owner, acting like a petulant child,
Defying his parents, like a bambino gone wild.

This boy pretender, with a heart so cold,
This spoiled young prince, doing damage untold.
He shot off his mouth all around town,
He was acting so resentful and frustrated,
Because he couldn't push Big Jim around;
And he could not be pacified or cajoled,
So, in terms of cow dung, he became quite a load!

We have so much pity for the Golden Gate City,
And the 49er Red and Gold.
Those brave young men, who are no longer so bold,
So recently ignored, and left out in the cold.
Y. A. Tittle commented very little,
While seeing the Whiners belittled.
He never thought it would end this way,
Nor did he ever think he would see the day!

FUTBOL

When you steal from your loyal fans,
Is it really a sin, or just a big scam?
It repeatedly feels, so incredibly grand,
When it's your country that usually wins,
One never tires of bragging amongst kin.
There are always lots of losers,
But there can only be one winner.
Some losers try to be the choosers,
They will oppose, act like accusers,
Change many of the original rules,
To become the profiteering new rulers,
Their only way to avoid being bad losers.

I see you are quite the beginner,
You have that desire to be a winner,
It will quickly make you a sinner,
It will blacken and ruin your soul,
Make your salvation much slimmer.
Most athletes have no personal desire
To become bold, bald-face liars.
They will not begrudge you your money,
They wish to excel for what is required.
They covet no one else's talents or skills,
They would not even attempt to steal,
Nor would they try to extort a bad deal.
Sadly, their Association has no integrity.
Who chooses these greedy celebrities?
All that they have ever managed to do,

From the exalted positions that they independently rule,
Manipulating schedules and telling deceitful lies,
Was cheating while taking extremely-exorbitant bribes!

I would not bear false witness,
Take bribes, cheat, or commit crimes;
But if you want to wallow in grime,
Go and get yourself ready to watch
Deluded, deceptive, double-crossing,
Scheduling manipulations contrived.
You can dole out
Little spoons of honey,
To those that come up with
The fast, easy money.
Commissioners caught gorging,
And acting like filthy swine.
Because once again, get ready,
It is International Futbol time!

HAWKS VS. LAMBS

Damn those Lambs!
Last time we really got slammed,
Scammed, jammed, flimflammed,
And rammed from behind.
They will find that this time,
We will not be so kind.
We will dominate their minds,
Their hands and their feet we will bind,
We are done fooling around with these guys.

Their players we will sideline,
And their drives we will unwind,
On their pride we will feast and dine,
No rest ever, for their Defensive Line.

This time we will not be fazed,
The fans will be crazed,

They may have to be tased,
That team will be totally amazed,
Razed, dazed,
Phased out and gone
Like the dawn,
Six feet under the lawn,
Just a ho-hum yawn,
The final pawn,
Really gone.

With a gasp and a scream,
A beaten team,
In the way of our dream,
With a full head of steam,
We will rise like the cream,
Straight to the very top,
We will not drop,
We will not stop,
On the Throne we will remain,
Yes sir, it will be the Hawks again!

McCLENDON ADDENDUM

Oh my, Heavens to Murgatroyd!
Oh how Seattle so loved Lloyd!
How well his players were deployed,
And how the umpires were so annoyed,
Those opposing bats that were destroyed,
And the new strategies that were employed.
Oh Lordy, Lordy, Lordy,
How Seattle so loved Lloyd!
Oh my, Heavens to Murgatroyd!

MR. AGGRESSIVE IN THE STRIKE ZONE

There is a fine young man
Of Major League, All-Star fame,
By his fans he is fondly called HoJo,
A shortened version of his name.
He was a switch-hitting Met's third baseman
And he played with a whole lot of game.

Now he's the Mariner's Batting Coach,
And also a very fine Baseball Spokesman!
At 2015 Spring Training I saw a young man,
Standing at the end of the Mariner's dugout.
Clutching a baseball, with his hand held out,
As it was taken by a good-looking, middle-aged man.

That is when I joined in,
With my eagerly-outstretched hand,
Me with a game ball,
Scuffed from hitting the stands.
He smiled a grin
And he carefully signed it,
Beautifully, just as if
He had designed it!

Truly he is,
What a Major League All-Star is all about,
Signing a couple of baseballs,
From underneath the dugout!

It took me all the way
Back to 1961,
When I would take the bus down
To Briggs' Tiger Stadium.
I was a ten-year-old with a
75-cent bleacher seat,
A bright-eyed young kid,
Always hoping to meet
Al Kaline and Norm Cash,
If you would please.
HoJo knowingly catered
To the innocent child in me.

And for that he will always
Hold my highest esteem.
And all about him,
I will publicly toast,
All across this nation,
And from coast-to-coast.
He's one of Major League Baseball's
Finest celebrity hosts!

That cherished treasure
Is stored in my safe,
The place where that baseball
Resides as of late.
Right next to all my
Precious pistols,
And my Wife's
Special jewelry.

It is kept very safe
From any tomfoolery.

Sometimes I bring out that baseball,
Just for all my friends to see,
And show them what a fine Gentleman
Howard Johnson was to me.

And my friends all
Knowingly smile,
As they all
Heartily do agree,
How he showed
A generous kindness
To a nostalgic
Old man like me.

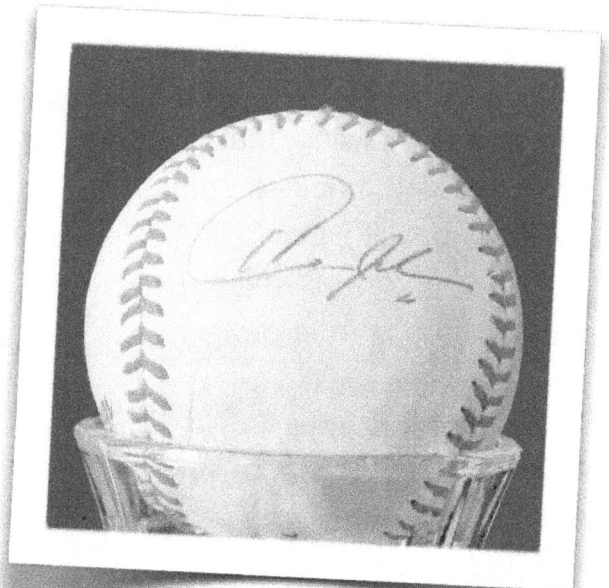

NFC CHAMPIONSHIP GAME 1/2015
SEATTLE SEAHAWKS VS. GREEN BAY PACKERS

Is it a Bay? Or really a Cay? I really can't say.
It is definitely green, from the manure that I've seen.
The odor is intense, and it makes their fans mean;
They are unable to smell their cheese and their beans.

The Hawks are Packer Trackers, not friendly backers,
But bona fide back-them-up, rack-them-up,
Stack-them-up, Jiu-Jitsu Back-Crackers.
They will jam them and jack them,
Really smack them and whack them.

The Seahawks are Packer Disasters
Who like to pound to the ground,
The Cheese Head team that flies
Into the glorious Puget Sound.

These cheesy Packer-Slackers,
These cud-chewing, teat-grabbing,
Curd-packing, back-slapping,
Ice-fishing, still-wishing-
For-those-good-old-days,
Of the Vince Lombardi ways.

Let them get serious,
Not so delirious.
Let them try if they can;
But down to the last man,
It is going to be their Last Stand.

The fans still think Rodgers,
Is a fleet Artful Dodger.
They're hoping that he possibly can
Come to the rescue
And be their Mr. Superman;
Such a tragic hope,
An incredible loss to their fans.

With his Ndamukong Suh bruise,
Sadly, he is about to lose.
In the spontaneous flash,
Of a photographer's pan,
This ass-kicking contest
Will be lost by a one-legged man.
Seattle will continue to be,
The most-favored home team,
Almost impossible to beat,
And the NFC Champion again!

After they fondue
This year's Green Bay Crew,
To no more be seen
In their yellow and green.
Gone is their struggling quest
To be the next "Very Best,"
And their unachievable goal,
To be at this year's Superbowl.

NORTH CAROLINA PANTHERS 2014

Seattle's wharf rats
Will scurry and scat,
As they leap into the sea,
To escape and be free,
Of the coming pungency.
It is such a foul and odiferous odor,
Slowly lofting and wafting all over
Our stunningly fine football stadium,
Fondly known to our Fans as The Clink;
Covered in a huge, billowing, aroma,
An invisible, malodorous, cloud of stink!

This is the land of the 12s,
On the grounds built from the Dome,
The place that the Hawks call Home,
It Is where they have always dwelled,
It is where their numbers have swelled.
Where the Hawks do not yield,
Where the home victory is sealed.
A place of swift death with a fist,
Where our field goals never miss,
Where the Cheerleaders blow you a kiss.

Very soon, most unfortunately,
Our pristine, venerated home field
Will likely be covered,
Literally quite-smothered,
In gallons of panicked,
North Carolina Panther piss!
180

OFFENSE

Some were still looking askance,
When they made Russell Wilson the Lance.
But when he goes into his elliptical trance,
And does his sure-footed, fast-moving dance,
He leads these Goliaths up on the front line,
Their strength and their timing, it just redefines.

Lunging right through your front door,
They add on another six-point score,
Very solid right through to the core,
So unlike any team you've seen before.
Can you really stop them? "Nevermore!"
Quoth Poe's Ravens from Baltimore.

The Beast is a battering ram,
He can bam, wham jam,
Oh man, he can really slam!
And he can cram,
And then you, he will tenderize and barbecue,
Slice you up like a honey ham.
Puree you just like strawberry jam!

This is not a scam.
When you see him coming,
While for him you go gunning,
But he hits you hard running.
It is like steel hitting a very large fan,
A dynamite blast to the front of a dam,

A nuclear bomb in the vast desert sands!
Receivers especially graceful and fast,
A most proficient and talented cast.
Like German Shorthairs' pointing noses,
Licking their lips, so perfectly focused
As they blast off to the point of attack.

They just want a chance,
To make the advance,
To prance right on by,
On a full tank of gas,

Our Receivers just rocket right past,
Their stunned rivals with flat feet,
They were just glued to the grass.
As the Pigskin flew past the Cornerback,
Into the hands of the Seahawk attack.

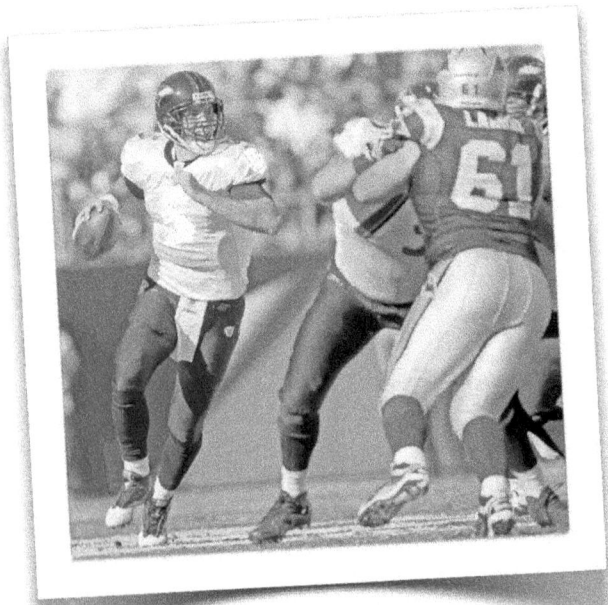

About the Tight Ends,
Oh, what can I say?
They risk bodies and minds,
Each day after day,
To block and to sock,
To blast by so fast,
Under the Goalpost's Double Mast,
For the sacrosanct Hail Mary Pass.

Wherefrom do these champions come,
Is it not your business to ask someone?
You should not really give out a behest,
Heed my words as you search in your quest,
And you most assuredly had better be scared,
When you glide into our Raptorial Nest!

If you come here to play football,
Soon you will be made to retreat,
Like the multi-colored Skittles,
Colorful fruit-flavored treats;
You are just food for our Beast!

PATRIOTS FANS

Historically your fans
Are some booze-smuggling gangs,
Some drunk, mugging thugs,
And some middle-class lugs.

Plus, those zealously-religious,
Not-so-spiritually ambitious,
Expeditiously-efficient dilettantes;
Those Boondocks' Saint Vigilantes.

But the worst of those charmers
Are those New England farmers;
They have the outward demeanor
Of sinister creatures, much meaner.
Callused hands covered in soot.
Those musty, crusty old codgers,

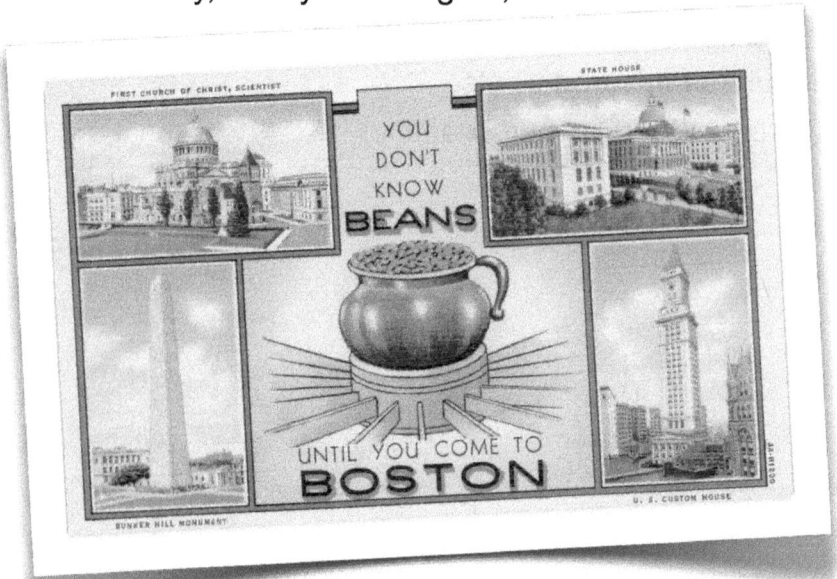

With manure on their boots;
Despising those weekend B & B lodgers.

Criticisms explicit, disheartening.
Chewing tobacco with only about half,
Of their yellow-stained teeth.
Hard-frozen, and caustically-mean,
Some of the crustiest old buzzards
That you folks have ever seen!

They just happen to make
Boston Beans look half-baked.
Not quite so homey and quaint,
Their outspoken comments
Without any restraint;
They can easily make
The daintier girls faint.

PATRIOTS' SCHISM

Who would have thought
That the Pats would get caught
At this late of a date;
Now we have Deflategate.

Who could anticipate
This nationwide debate
On the ethical state
Of the New England Patriots?

And now it does seem
That their Superbowl Dreams
Shall blow up in their face.
Geez, what a disgrace!

I just couldn't make,
Not even *think* to create,
Of such a plan to deflate.

A poorly-thought scheme,
It has spoiled their Dream,
To be history's best team!

The scheme utterly denigrates,
But the Hawks will not shirk,
When they take down the Patriots.

Bringing their lunch pails to work,

They will pound, cut and shear,
While the 12s drink their beer.

Quickly annihilate,
Delicately eviscerate.
These fakes, these cakes,
These flakes, these rakes;
Lots of skullduggery,
From the six Yankee States.

Whose only main claim to fame,
That New England could say,
They were Honest and True Blue,
And followed The Golden Rule.

But they thought they could fool;
Which makes them to blame.
So sad, what a contemptible shame
That they have brought to the Game!

They will lie and deny,
As they have many times.
But there is no blue sky
For these Patriot crimes.

Their fans have been covered
In their slime and their grime;
And most likely this time,
They will pay a Big Fine.

The sky is not falling
On this NFL mauling.
For every good drama
Needs some kind of trauma.
And someone who is willing
To be the bad villain.
It will raise all of the national TV ratings
While the rest of the country is expatriating.

As the interest increases
Raw emotion releases.
And basically it's funny;
Execs make more money,
Yet they act all depressed.
Yes, it is what you have guessed.

What the public did miss—
What the truth really is—
Is that the big money gamblers
Are pathetically, psychotically pissed!

(Aw, Hell, all that and they *still* won the game!)

PERSECUTION OF THE BEAST

Dodger From Hell, you are one wicked Prick,
And a perfect reflection of the Rich Owners' schtick.
Why are you maiming the Hero of us all,
And despoiling our beloved game of Football?

Your persecution of our Beast
Was so juvenile, so predictable.
Entirely undeniable, and yet inconceivable.
Very reprehensible, really unforgivable.
Stupefyingly stupid, and unbelievable.
Totally unsupportable, so publicly disrespectable.
Highly embarrassable, ethically unjustifiable.
Cro-Magnon-like behavior, totally unreasonable.

An oppressor, a tyrant, a mogul;
Dodger From Hell, you are a bitter pill.
Your harassment of the Beast, inch by inch,
It is a most disagreeable pinch.

You are viciously inflexible,
Most incredibly unlikable.
Disobliging, petulant, and ungracious;
But essentially indefensible and salacious.
You are on top of a cup brimming full,
Of Politically-Correct dogmatic Bull!

PRE-SMACK SUPERBOWL XLIX
PATRIOTS VS. SEAHAWKS

Those war-painted Indian imitators,
Those Tea Party, tax-dodging instigators,
Those revolutionary, disloyal, perpetrators;
What is this Boston bunch all about?

These bean-baking,
Lobster-eating,
Samuel Adams-drinking,
Fine-wine-tasting,
Hoity-toity,
Pinkie-waving,
Deep sea yacht-sailing,
Funny crow-speaking louts.
This is a scream!

There is not very much
That this Boston bunch
Can hope to surmount,
When they meet on the green.
And after they've seen
The Men Without Doubt,
From the West, not the South,
With their Legion of Boom,
Who will soon seal their doom!

The Pats will make their last stand
In the burning hot sands,
When the Hawks take command
Of this hostile land,
While also controlling
The fans in the stands.

Historically your fans
Are some booze-smuggling gangs,
And some drunk-mugging thugs,
And some middle-class lugs;
Plus those zealously-religious,
Spiritually-ambitious,
Expeditiously-efficient,
Vigilante-type,
Boondock Saints.

Again we mention those suave, savvy charmers,
Those witch-hunting New England farmers;

They have the outward demeanor
Of sinister creatures, much meaner
Which makes all the young girls faint.

So to all of these Puritan People Of Late,
To these East Coast Yankees,
In six different states,
Right here and right now I can state,
We do not have much to relate,
So again what I have left to reiterate:
The Pats have a dismal date with their Fate.

It is so sad, but I have a hunch
That no one's feeling bad
For that slap-happy 'Shady Bunch,'
Nor for 'The Shrek' you mean
Nor that crusty old troll,
Grumpy 'Will Pain In The Neck!'

Boston will pout all about,
The coming rout in this bout.
Do not be so glum,
Do not be so dumb,
We really don't care,
Wherefrom you do come.

Nor how old your ancestors are, my Son,
Nor wherefrom before, of yore, ye come,
Because when all is said and done,

We will have already begun,
To dismantle these Yankee Bums,
With our Northwest Young Guns,
In the blinding-bright
Arizona-stadium lights.

No one will be stopping or topping
Our jaw-dropping,
Superbowl Run!

THE CURSE OF SAFECO FIELD

The new stands were so grand,
And the concourses sweeping;
Food and beverage dispensers
Were sterile and in keeping.

With a higher, elevated level
Of upscale ballpark cuisine,
Everything was so brand spanking new,
It was all so sparkling and clean!

It was the House that Ken Griffey built,
And with Edgar and the Bone,
The Mariners now had
An exceptionally-good home.
There was hope and a future
For the faithful Mariners Fans,

And they soon would be filling
Those large, empty stands.
Before Safeco Field opened
On July 15th, 1999,
There was a nefarious horror show unfolding,
For our unsuspecting, loyal Mariners Fans
Clueless till now, but very soon to understand.

A construction worker, a lackey, a shirker,
Like a troll, caught with a shovel under the stars working,
An evildoer, skulking and maliciously lurking;
The Suspect hanging around the job site very late,
Up to skullduggery, near our future home plate.

The investigation was about to astound.
Sadly what was officially recovered,
Buried five feet deep in the ground;
A dirty old Red Sox uniform was found!

The contaminated garment was not returned;
Unceremoniously, it was promptly burned,
To destroy Boston's ancient Old Bambino Curse,
From hiding in Seattle's infield dirt.

That reprobate worker was fired,
Quickly, most swiftly, without fail.
He should have been tarred and feathered,
Then run out of town on a rail!
Heading back east, he hit the trail,
Before someone could ring his bell,
Down that short Highway to Hell.

He was very lucky indeed,
Not to have slowly been drowned,
In the very dark, shadowy-green waters
Of the deep and icy-cold Puget Sound!

As a result of his actions,
I truly may fear,
You should never consider to ever wear,
That Most-Despised Boston Red Sox Gear.

Whenever a Boston fan
Is publicly wearing his gear
And he randomly, unknowingly,
Just happens to appear,
The locals get angry,
And send out the loud jeers.

It is the least welcome of all,
I would not give you a bum steer.
Because no one will ever
Want to buy you a beer,
If you are stupidly wearing
Any Despicable Red Sox Gear!

As a result, what we most seemed to hear,
Was that for over these many, many baseball years,
The long ball mysteriously just seemed to disappear.
We brought in Big Boppers, from all over the Realm,
And a bevy of new Managers, came to the helm;
But we just could not seem to extricate,
That damned Demon Curse from our own home plate.

The Diamond Club
At Safeco Field
Has made a new home for
The Babe, they feel.
They hope he
Likes his new digs,
And has decided to stay,
Because his House in New York,
Sadly, has now gone away.

We hoped he battled that Demon right off of the plate,
Sent him right back to his infamous, sinister fate:
Back to 4 Yawkey Way, at the old Fenway Park,
Back to where he belongs, where he had his big start.

If you still have your doubts,
If you don't believe what I'm saying,
Visit Safeco Field, just go out,
Where the Mariners are playing.
The lack of cracking of bats,
And no visible tipping of hats,
Will show you the Babe's Curse,
Never left, it never went back.
That great baseball player,
We all hold so dear,
Had his curse relocated,
It's a Poltergeist not sated!

This blasphemy is putting a jinx
On the players' psyches, I think.
We need a good Catholic Priest,

One that is really an Exorcist,
To make the ball carry further,
Into Elliot Harbor's seaside mist!

To get the Ms back in gear,
So the fearful fans once again
Can rejoice and happily cheer,
Let me buy you a nine-dollar beer,
To catch our continuously-falling,
Abundant amounts of sobbing tears!

THIRD BASE SHINING STAR

A bright Young Star did arise,
With piercing, icy-blue eyes.
A purebred Golden Retriever,
An early-to-rise Eager Beaver,
Who goes by the name Kyle Seager;
He has made us all into believers.

With his glove and his bat,
He always puts up great stats,
Covers the field like a cat,
Throws to First, so exact.

The truth will be told,
Your eyes do not lie,
He is a genuine All-Star,
Not any one person can deny!

Seniority

DECLINING YEARS

I do not have much time.
That is the reason why,
I lucidly define,
These waning years
Of my steady decline;
My retreating fitness,
By God's Premier Design.

The pieces no longer
Easily fall into place.
I've developed more wrinkles
All over my face.
My ability to heal
Cannot keep up the pace.

I cannot drink, I cannot smoke.
So lucky I am still able to toke.
Don't laugh, please don't chuckle,
It is not a whimsical joke!

If I put a little hot sauce on the side,
My bowels turn into a water slide.
The faint of heart cannot abide
This downward-spiral coaster ride.

Can't eat, can't sleep—
Dear God, so sweet—
I have such very tender feet.

Digestion stinks,
My penis shrinks,
Muscles atrophy
Like sausage links.

More and more I must despair,
My head keeps losing silky hair.
My ears and back, it's growing there.
My memory is gone, I don't know where.
My enlarging ass keeps getting flat.
Can't touch my toes, can't bend my back.

My skin so easily pinches and tears,
Scratched only slightly, a red rash appears.
It is effortlessly easy to break the skin,
It just keeps on getting so very thin.
So easily it burns, when out in the sun,
All covered up on the beach
While just trying to have fun.

Frustration brings
My blurry eyes to tears.
But I can't complain,
I've had a lot of good years.
My yellowing teeth are almost done.
I am always flossing, it is not much fun.
Stained ivory makes me hide my grins,
While life tallies up my bodily sins.
All of those years are catching up,
I still don't care, I'm not giving up!

When we near my Lonely Whistle Stop,
My train comes chugging round the bend.
I've come down off the mountaintop,
As my downhill journey nears its end.

About me, I hope the Good Lord
Does not want to give up,
Or hold back my reservation
For my home up above.
A jubilant place en route to ascend,
A place in eternity, forever, no end.

I now hope I have done well, scoring high on this test,
Although not always performing, at my very best.
There is one thing for sure, and I do not jest,
Someday I will finally get a full night's rest!

ENJOY A FEW DRINKS
WITH MY FAVORITE THINGS

New lyrics for My Favorite Things, 1959
written by Richard Rodgers and Oscar Hammerstein,
performed by Julie Andrews in "The Sound of Music"

Rainbows and sunshine and bright-blooming flowers,
Dark chocolate, clean sheets, and super hot showers,
Coffee, fresh donuts, egg custard so sweet,
Time to get happy, enjoy a few drinks!

Beachfront vacations, a bake shop's sweet fragrance,
Crisp Fish n' Chips, then the Friday-night dances,
Fresh chicken salad, mud trucks that won't sink,
Time to get happy, enjoy a few drinks!

White wine with shrimp pasta, baseball and football,
Cabernet wine, ribeyes, and waiters on call,
Fast cars and old bars, and girls dressed in pink,
Time to get happy, enjoy a few drinks!

CHORUS:
When the rent's due, and the car tanks,
Doctor bills unpaid.
Grin and get happy, enjoy a few drinks—
It keeps me from feeling sad!

I'M SO RETIRED

Sung to the tune "I'm So Excited"
By The Pointer Sisters and Trevor Lawrence, 1982

Three years ago, it finally did happen.
To my place of work, I gladly said "Goodbye!"
Kicked up my heels, my fingers were a-snappin',
I'm just so glad I managed to survive!

CHORUS:
I want to leave you,
Heave you,
I really want to choke you.
I want to dump you,
Junk you,
I've had about enough.
So pay me all my dough,
And I will go.

I'm so retired,
Glad I can't get fired.
I'm about to hit the road,
And I am ecstatic.
I'm so retired,
Glad I can't get fired.
I won't show
Won't show
Won't show
Won't show.

I hate you!
I hate you!

Happily thinking, all about tomorrow,
I get to leave this bullshit all behind.
I'll get my check, get out within the hour,
I'm so glad to leave this Boring Daily Grind.

CHORUS:
I'm so retired,
Glad I can't get fired.
I'm about to hit the road
And I am ecstatic.
I'm so retired,
Glad I can't get fired.
I won't show
Won't show
Won't show
Won't show
Won't show
I hate you!
I hate you!

I want to leave you,
Heave you,
I really want to choke you.
I want to dump you,
Junk you,
I've had about enough.
So pay me all my dough,

And I will go.
I'm so retired,
Glad I can't get fired.
I'm about to hit the road
And I am ecstatic.

I'm so retired,
Glad I can't get fired.
I won't show
Won't show
Won't show
Won't show
Won't show
I hate you!
I hate you!

I'm so ignited.
Finally will be free.
Just can't deny it.
You got me burning up.
I'm about to hit the road,
And I know I like it.
I'm so delighted.
I want to leave you.
I'm so incited.
Look what you've done to me,
You've had me churning up.
I'm so done with you!

LONGER NIGHTS

I'm getting much closer towards the end of the year,
Fond memories of summer, we all hold so dear.
Dropping leaves, Mother Nature is moving ahead—
Autumn yellows, lots of oranges, and also bright reds,
Eventually then turning a dark, crispy brown;
Each day getting older, my leaves dropping down.

It was a good year;
Everything that transpired
I really hold dear.
I grew up in the spring,
Trying to learn everything.
I fully matured in the summer,
Just learning to be a good lover.

Of all of God's gifts, of all growing things,
Spreading my branches, like albatross wings.
Protecting all from the sun and the wind,
Trying to forgive the ones who have sinned.
Blessing the sun and the clouds and the rain,
Personal growth, healthy, free of all pain.

The days quickly diminish,
As the nights become longer.
My job's almost finished,
My legacy becomes stronger.

With the arrival of the cold winter winds,
Who knows?
Maybe next year,
The Cosmos will let me do it again.

TRADE-OFFS

Lately these days, since I have retired,
(An achievement I have always desired),
I have come to a sobering realization,
A discovery of a very new frustration.

A total lifestyle change has been required;
Unbeknownst to me, I'm becoming rewired.
I have had to adjust to much more isolation,
It's a trade-off we make, for more civilization.

Not so dependent on my family and friends,
Our freedom of choice, is what this country defends.
So on to new places, around the country I roamed,
If I became homesick, there was always a phone.

Happily I married, a young lady friend,
We fell for each other, and left the Stay Single trend.
Just us, we raised our two young cubs all alone,
Desperately we financed, a small modest home.

Without family and friends, it was tough,
Financial sacrifice, very often was rough.
For a new climate, a new land, I made a trade;
Little time to make friends, was the price that I paid.

Kids raised through college, was reward quite enough.
We had all of the basics, we did not need the fluff.
I have no regrets for the choices I've made,

For all of the effort, for all of those bills that we paid.

Now that I'm in my Golden Years,
Cautiously now, I must count all my beers.
I have very few hobbies, and very few friends,
So I spend time alone, carefully seeking my Zen.

And now I must deal, with those late-in-life fears,
Of all I've done wrong, it can bring me to tears!
My flaws and my failures, I cannot defend,
I cannot go back, and make my amends.

Whether it is going to heaven, or reincarnation,
It seems to make sense, that we have destination.
Seems that my shortage of friends and sociable drinkers,
Has left me with much more free time,
To be a Great Thinker.

To ponder my deepening fascination,
With the Great Spirit's Purpose
For all of Creation.
Maybe it's the meditation,
That created this connection,
But I've made a new friend,
And he has a great Ascension!

WHAT IS THE MEASURE?

Oftentimes I contemplate
My spiritual state,
My distant fate,
That future date,
With those Pearly Gates.
I theorize about who I was and who I am,
And if now, I am a better man.
The question is, as it was presented to me—
"Will I exist, and will I still be able to see?"

As the beat in my heart starts to cease,
When family and friends witness me
Failing to breath subconsciously,
I will wonder if Life was really a test.
And did I do, my very best?
While pondering these thoughts in my head,
Of denial and personal dread,
When everything is all done and said,
The question remains: "Is there life after death?"

And is that truly what Jesus said?
It is such a huge conflict,
Between the trust and the doubt;
No peace of mind,
No small amount.

Religion and philosophy,
Neither one can prove to me,

Nor do they have the ability
To reveal resurrection or divinity;
Visually, audibly, in reality,
Or in a physical sensitivity.

We want the Big Picture,
So we can truly understand,
Just exactly who we are,
And wherefrom we come,
And what is the Big Plan.

Our conception to redemption,
Everything that we're about,
And it keeps me always flooded,
With a lot of personal doubt.

When my soul seeks a free release,
I hope that I can find my Peace.
I will always wonder
What is in my cup,
And if I will truly measure up.

I am a man of my word,
With my handshake as my bond,
That is the style, of which I am fond.

I try to be kind, and extend a strong hand.
I am always willing to lend someone a tool,
Until they try to use me like a fool.
Occasionally generous, whenever I can,
With no special message that I was trying to send.

There was nothing that I was trying to prove,
It just seemed like it was the right thing to do.

When in my youth,
I forsook Moses' Truths;
It seemed easier to survive.
And although I strived,
I really did not thrive.
And sometimes I was lucky,
Just to end up safe and alive.

I changed my location,
And I made a fresh start.
I found a decent job,
And I got a better car.
I made honesty the best policy,
Out of the gate from the start.
And it opened all of the doors,
To the nice people's hearts.

Now that I'm older and wiser, I think,
I look for some wisdom, to wisely impart.
So this is the key secret, I am sharing for free:
"Just make sure you hang on to your honesty."

So other than that, that is all that there is,
I have nothing more, nothing more than I did before.
No more to impart, than I had from the start;
That is the truth, laser-straight from my heart.
I will always wonder, how full is my cup,
And if I will truly, in my final days, measure up.

WINTER YEARS

I think about my Winter Years,
Review my life, the happy times,
Retrospective joyful tears,
Successful pride is so sublime.

Spring so jubilantly appears,
Carefree children, gleeful nursery rhymes,
Mother's cures for those dreadful fears,
Innocence, hope, exciting finds.

Summertime's the Young Adult Years,
Taking chances, committing crimes,
Learning from mistakes, one matures,
Finding love, life's future designs.

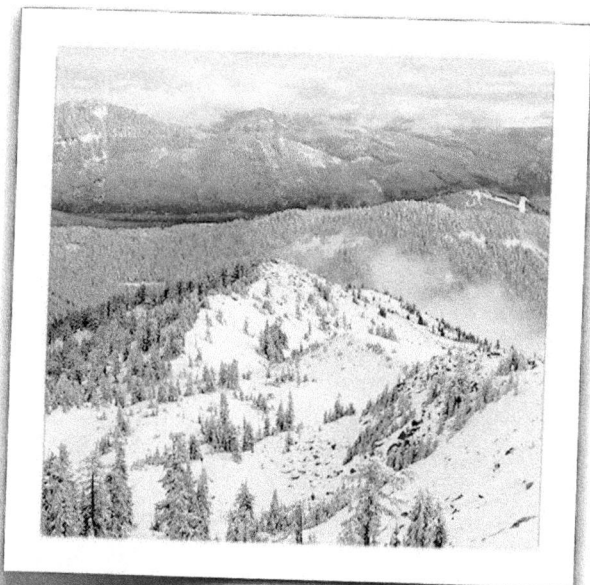

Autumn is like the Middle Years,
The bells of time begin to chime,
Accomplishments, downshifting gears,
Casually energetic, enterprise declines.

Crystal winter is the Golden Years,
My bounteous Creator, has been so kind,
Will the Golden Gates suddenly reappear,
Or will I reoccur, to another Springtime?

Travel Epics

FORT LAUDERDALE
AND THE EVERGLADES

I arrived in Fort Lauderdale in June of 1968.
I was sixteen and I had
Just finished eleventh grade
With Big Muscles Sam,
And Crazy Lebanese Teddy,
Along with wide-body,
Southern-Fried Bubba;
Teddy liked to call me
"Little Skinny Blondie."

What these guys already knew,

As a matter of fact, was that
I just happened to be very lean.
And the truth of the matter was that
I had decent, very strong muscles.
But sadly, so sorrowfully,
They just didn't bulge or buff out,
Undefined, subtle, not-fully grown;
Even though they worked very well,
They were shy, and hadn't yet shown!

Although we were only in High School,
We had gone to Florida on Spring Break!
We had left in Bubba's old camper pick-up truck,
For gas, we had all chipped in, it was great!
We had had a good trip, it had all been quite a ball,
Now back in Michigan, we took a Florida phone call.

We were now hired for all of the summer
To detail Bill Binko's New and Used Cars;
Cleaning them up meticulously for resale.
Buffing them bright, shiny and sharp,
Working for Bubba's Uncle Barney,
And his sweet, lovely wife Martha,
With their five fun, fabulous kids,
Who graciously made room for us all,
Until we would be returning to school,
For the beginning of the quarter in Fall.

Barney owned a genuinely,
Substantially ample,
Roomy and large gas station,
With a sizable tire selection,
In an excellent, beachfront location.
Doing it all, in a three-car stall;
A Chevron, Full-Service Station,

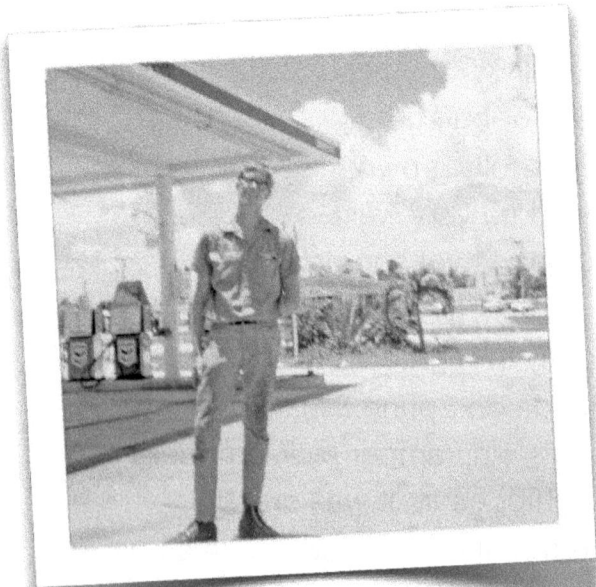

With a large, hefty tow truck,
Just in case that your automobile
Suddenly became down on its luck.

It was parked right out in front,
And that became my new job,
Jump-starting batteries and changing flat tires,
Also towing the broken down cars,
Whatever the situation required,
Back to the gas station parking lot.

I was proud that Barney trusted me,
Even though I was still only sixteen,
They showed so much faith and trust;
I was somewhat amazed and shocked.
And I was very careful not to mess up!

It was a very short trip
That you could easily walk
To the famous Bill Binko
Chrysler-Dodge Dealership.
Genuinely, quite-literally, over the top,
The Nation's second most-voluminous,
Monumentally-large and spacious,
The selection was totally outrageous;
It was a gigantic dealership parking lot.

We had to work side-by-side
With these two Negro guys,
Who spoke uncommonly fast,
With overly-strong accents.

They came from the ghetto,
From underneath the Palmettos,
In deep, Deep South Miami;
That was really about all,
That Barney could tell me.

I did not mind being trained
By these two good-natured guys,
Even though I was from the North.
And Detroit was still racially separated,
It was all completely segregated;
Very similar to the traditional South,
Detroit was not at all integrated.
My own experiences were the exception,
I was already racially amalgamated.
My Grandparents' home was Downtown,
Which my Great-Grandfather had built
With his own Canadian hardworking hands;
To this day, a miracle, that it still stands.
A humble two-story brick home,
Now in a ghetto on Twelfth Street, all alone.

Since then dedicated, and famously renamed,
It is called Rosa Parks Boulevard.
It is not far from Bagley Street,
Where Henry Ford had started his first factory.
Only a few blocks away, not too very far,
Down near the slow-moving Detroit River.
Standing so proud then, was the old coliseum,
The Tigers' most inconspicuously-named
Briggs' Major League Baseball Stadium.

224

Where I think I was the only white kid,
(And a towhead, at that!)
For about a two-mile radius,
In every direction, all around;
I was the only one downtown
That could likely be found.

And I was the only one,
Of the four of us teens,
Used to segregation in Michigan,
Who was comfortable enough
To work side-by-side with Black Men.
Only I had any experience
With Negro relations,
With not-yet-to-come
Racial Integration.

These two easy-going, very-private black guys,
In their middle-twenties, with big, wide smiles,
They would speak un-intelligible English,
We could not possibly deduce or decipher.
Nothing that I could possibly translate;
Only finger pointing would elucidate.
They did not read anything,
And they did not write, either.
What they were speaking,
I could understand neither.
An impenetrable version,
Of a deep, Deep-Southern drawl;
No one could understand them at all!

Barney said,"Don't even bother.
I grew up around here,
And I cannot hardly fathom,
Their unique language at all.
Just observe and watch them,
Then they will point out for you,
Everything that you need to do.
I'm sure it will all work out.
So relax and stay cool,
If you will be understanding,
They will be accommodating,
To amicably teach all to you."

Well, Big Sam and Teddy
Just did not have a clue what to do.
They were very good at sports,
Lifting weights and street fighting,
But for them, working in general,
And especially polishing used cars.
It did not take the boys very long,
Before they were quickly deciding,
They did not like having a job;
For them it was tedious and unexciting.
At night they took off
To the neighborhood McDonald's
Just on the other side of the tracks,
Looking for trouble, trying to pick fights
With some of the local blacks.
Until one of those young men,
Stuck a gun directly into their faces;
He had put those two knuckleheads

Back into their lunatic places.

Now they were not happy,
And they wanted to go home.
Bubba was used to being spoiled
By his Mother and Grandmother;
Not used to being out on his own.
But Barney's wife, Martha,
Was not having any of it;
So the boys swiftly decided
They were going back home.
Barney said I could stay,
If I did not want to go.
So I said,"Oh Hell, yeah,
I am perfectly willing
To let those lazy bums go!"
Barney's cool swimming pool,
So rare in those days;

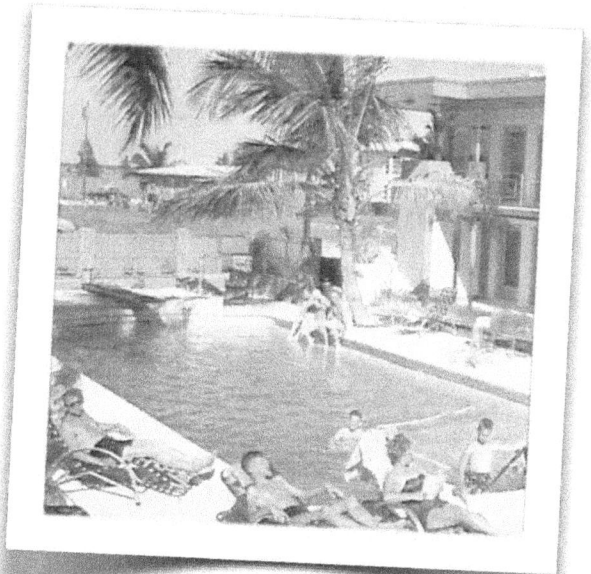

That was all the more reason
For me to stay and appreciate.

The fortuitous circumstances,
Of my new current situation,
I was enjoying it all,
No frustration, no agitation!
Detailing cars, inside the gas station.

What was really a blast from the past,
Was the affluent subdivision in back.
A wealthy, gated community,
Between US Highway Number 1
And the white, sandy beach;
Going in through the back way,
It was all very easy to reach.

This was where Johnny Weissmuller,
The most famous of Tarzans,
Spent his Florida winters
Deep-sea fishing for Tarpon.
Seems he'd gotten himself hooked
On the warm, tropical winds,
So he left the hills of Hollywood
For Florida's beaches of white sands.

His career had been grand!
But he was now retired;
He spent much of his time
Drinking fine wine,
Eating crackers and Brie,

Enjoying his long winters,
With other famous celebrities.

The neighborhood streets,
Paved smooth without fault,
Covered in a very silky, sleek,
Black, brand-new asphalt.
The streets were banked in the turns,
A perfect place for a young kid to learn.
Because everyone - the well-to-do,
The moneyed, that prosperous brood -
They flew away for the summer;
For me, it was all so especially good!
I could freely race cars, without any stops,
Through that desolate neighborhood;
No one was living there, to call any cops.
I had access to drive,
Every kind of used car.
Corvettes and Camaros,
Mustangs, Alfa Romeos.
Mercedes and Jaguars,
And all of Dodge-Chrysler's
Brand-new line of Muscle Cars.

As soon as those cars,
Came off of the trucks,
We would wash off the dirt,
Protective wax was polished off.
I would check the oil and the gas,
Then I would take the cars for a run.
Damn, it was a whole lot of fun!

Plymouth Barracudas,
Plymouth Road Runners,
Dodge 440 Magnums,
And Dodge HEMI Chargers.

For my personal transportation,
If I had a date, or somewhere to go,
Barney would loan me a rebuilt
1959 Chrysler DeSoto.
If I had to run any special errands,
He would give me a holler;
Like driving to the nearby 7-Eleven,
With one single dollar,
For an ice-cold watermelon.
He would toss me the keys,
To his brand-new Cadillac,
And he would say to me,
"Please, bring it on back
All complete, unscratched,
And in just one piece."

Things even got better, you see,
How I looked forward
To all of the weekends;
I never had time to get bored.
Barney and Martha would pack up the kids,
Along came the old carpenter Omar,
Who was most fondly called Gomer.
He would show up early and join in,
Helping us to load the storage bins.

We would pack up the camper,
Heading out for bass fishing.
The camper was made,
From a Cadillac limousine;
With an acetylene torch,
It was cut off behind the front seat.
Barney had built a six-sleeper camper,
On top of the limousine frame, incredibly.
On the back was a six-foot square table,
On hinges that would fold down easily,
Revealing a complete, fully-loaded,
Old-style, Chuck Wagon kitchen,
Complete with a propane gas stove.

On top we would tie down
The 12-foot aluminum skiff.
To the hitch on the back of the limo
We would hook up the boat trailer,
Loaded with the 24-foot wooden boat.
Then we would get on the highway,
Heading directly due west;

It was called the Tamiami Trail,
And it was straight as an arrow.
At ninety miles an hour,
We were going Hell's Bells!

We would get to our favorite campground,
Wanting to launch boats in the water so late.
One had to watch out for poisonous snakes,
That were out there, lurking and skulking.

At night just wearing flip-flops while walking,
Watching out for various species of snakes,
We would do some intense water patrolling,
Scanning the unbroken surface for creatures lolling,
Very deliberate and completely sober,
Looking for any ripples out in the water.
We had to make sure that the area was safe,
Before unloading the boats into the lake.

We rose up very early the next morning,
Climbed in to the boats and started trolling.

Speaking of poisonous water snakes,
There were two or three kinds in the lake.
During those summer excursions
We killed 21 deadly serpents;
These events were always exciting diversions.

There were a few alligators
But they were protected.
(They were almost hunted
To extinction for their leather.)
Sometimes we would accidentally catch,
A sharp-toothed Garfish, instead of a Bass.

We would save them on the stringer
And give them to the old Black ladies
Who were always fishing
With 16-foot cane poles,
In their folding lawn chairs,
Along the sides of the river.

One time, we spotted an Indian camp,
Probably the Miccosukee,
Who lived in the swamp.
One of the original Seminole Tribes,
Not transplanted from Oklahoma,
These are Ancient Natives I describe.
With campfires burning,
Not far from the canal,

I jumped out of the boat
To meet them and introduce myself.
Barney and Gomer were yelling at me -
"What the Hell are you doing?
If you go and walk into that camp,
We can assuredly guarantee you,
That you will not ever come back!"
I said, "Alright, guys, calm down,
I can fully appreciate that."

While fishing in the skiff one time,
I confronted a four-foot alligator.
I had him trapped between the bank
And the side of the aluminum boat.
We were having very intense combat,
On the side of the muddy riverbank;
I had a wooden paddle in my left hand
And I shoved down hard on his throat.
Just as I was able to get close,
Reaching for jaws with my right hand,
He would always manage to spin,
Rolling over and over again.
I had to be prudently careful.
Eventually I thought I was going
To wear him down and take him;
But he won the Battle Royale.
I had to congratulate him,
On totally tuckering me out;
It was a battle I just couldn't win.

I did not want to lose my fingers,

To that fast-snapping, toothy snout.
I got tired and bored,
So I pushed the boat out,
Away from the shore.
Watched him quickly disburse,
Into the muck and the murk.

One time we drove to this restaurant
Shrouded deep in the Everglades.
The sign over the door said:
"If Your Heart Ain't In Dixie, Get Your Ass Out!"
Behind the back of the restaurant
Was an extensive marina of docks.
There must at least have been
Somewhere between 50 and 60
Propeller airboats that were moored therein.
Inside there were lots of rattlesnake skins,
Stretched out thin and nailed to the walls.
Alligators were Federally protected;
None of those were displayed there at all;
To hunt gators was totally restricted.

Within the last two years,
Four or five Federal Agents
Mysteriously had disappeared.
All the boatmen wore camouflage;
It looked like a movie from Vietnam.
They carried high-powered rifles with scopes,
Including their side arms and machetes;
They looked like they were ready for action, no joke!
They hunted gators at night

With high-powered spotlights.
Aimed the crosshairs in-between
Those two big, reflective eyes.
Most all of those guys,
Looked pretty scary and mean.
It was the most amazing place
That I had ever before seen.

Another story I have to tell:
Fishing in a cay, off of the canal,
Climbing up the ladder for the maintenance man,
Onto this old, moss-enshrouded concrete dam.
With only my swimsuit covering my buns,
Fishing from on top of the ledge in the sun,
Looking down into the shadowy abyss,
I had found a bountiful school of fish.

I was catching very large crappies,
I was stocking up, getting happy.
Filling my stringer as fast as I could,
All it took was the proficient speed,
With which to re-bait my hook.
For entertainment, I was flicking the end
Of that tip on my fishing pole,
Whipping at the four-inch-wide-diameter
Yellow-Green, blue, and red spiders.
Oblivious, not being very cautious,
To avoid picking up hitchhiking riders;
I was too absorbed in the fishing instead.

Gomer cruised up to the dam
236

In the aluminum skiff.
Then he said,"What in the Hell are you doing?"
I said, "I got into a big school of crappies!"
Gomer said,"You idiot! You're a damned fool,
Those spiders are extremely poisonous!"

Here I was standing barefoot,
Only wearing my bathing suit,
Completely surrounded,
By giant, pissed-off spiders,
Desperately hanging on to the shreds,
Of their freshly-torn and tattered webs.
I had not really considered
That I could have, so sadly,
Ended up cold, gray and dead.
I carefully extricated myself,
This time I moved a little bit faster;
Hastily and daintily away from,
A potential Arachnid Disaster.

Thinking I could stay in Ft. Lauderdale,
I went to visit the public school.
I was intending just to register,
For my senior year in high school.
But unknowingly I had been a fool.
As an underage citizen existing in Florida,
There was absolutely no such thing
As emancipated minors living independently.
I just wanted to be allowed to be free.
But the Principal said, "If you do not return home,
It is most important that I mention,

That you will be entering
Into a year-long juvenile detention."

Now experiencing my first plane ride,
Dejectedly I flew on back home.
It was not where I wanted to reside,
My Father was most difficult to abide.

I returned to my High School
For my final Senior Year,
To my friends and my teachers,
That I held very dear!
But my exciting, great adventure in Florida
That summer,
Was a fantastic experience
I will always remember!

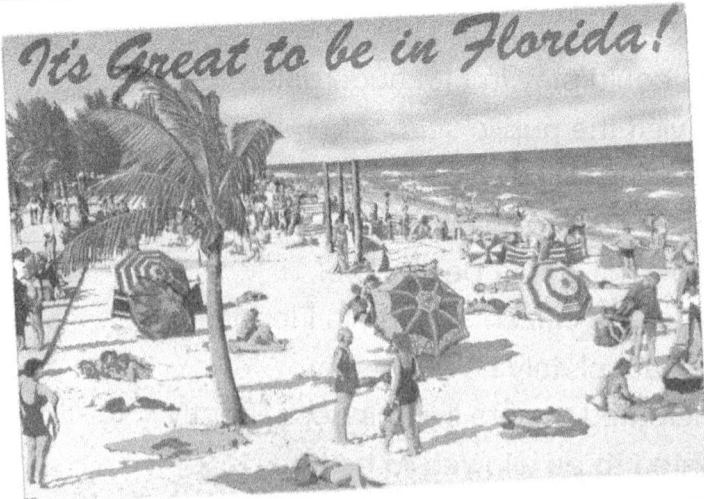

It's Great to be in Florida!

WEST BY NORTHWEST TO ALASKA

1 EVACUATE, ESCAPE AND EMIGRATE

In 1969 we had dreams and imagination.
Our graduation was an exciting expectation,
Of a glorious summer, of travels and exploration.
We were deciding on a fortuitous destination,
Spring sprouting speciously with speculation;
Moving up fast, was our graduation celebration.

We were making considerable plans,
We were going to travel to new lands,
Time to break out the brass band!
Not just leaving for the summertime;
We had no intentions of returning, anytime.

Larry and I had purchased
Bubba's old Dodge pick-up;
An old beat-up, camper truck.
I think we had paid
About three hundred bucks.

I installed some rebuilt springs,
And we bought some new tires.
I gave it a tune-up,
And repaired damaged wires.

We had a case of instant coffee,
Bought lots of canned and dry goods;
We seriously had thought,

That it was more than plenty of food.
Larry had a 303 Springfield rifle,
We each had .22 scoped rifles;
I had a brand new Remington
12-gauge pump-action shotgun.
We were leaving Detroit, Michigan,
And we didn't think we would ever
Be returning back home again.
All of our relationships, forever,
We were about to cut and sever.

We wanted out of the suburbs.
We thought we wanted to be
Just like Outdoor Mountain Men;
A childish teenage fantasy.
Flourishing in the Great Outdoors,
It had a lot of romantic allures.

I was thinking of fishing and surfing in Mexico;
The reality, just a white peasant with a row boat.
But Larry was very adamant,
He would not even consider it.
Now as I'm looking back upon it,
That was the smart intelligent decision;
One can't make much money in Mexico fishing.
It was a good thing
That we didn't show,
Way down south in Mexico.
There was so much
About crime and such,
That we just didn't know;

It was fatefully prudent,
That we decided not to go!

Larry said, "North to Alaska,
That is where it is the best;
Better than all of the rest!
The good hunting and fishing,
The great camping and trapping,
It is the summit, the pinnacle,
Unquestionably, without peer
America's Last Wild Frontier."

The major epitomic domicile,
Of all things virgin and wild;
A gigantic wilderness undefiled.
All of the Outdoorsmen know,
Alaska is the Really Big-Time Show!

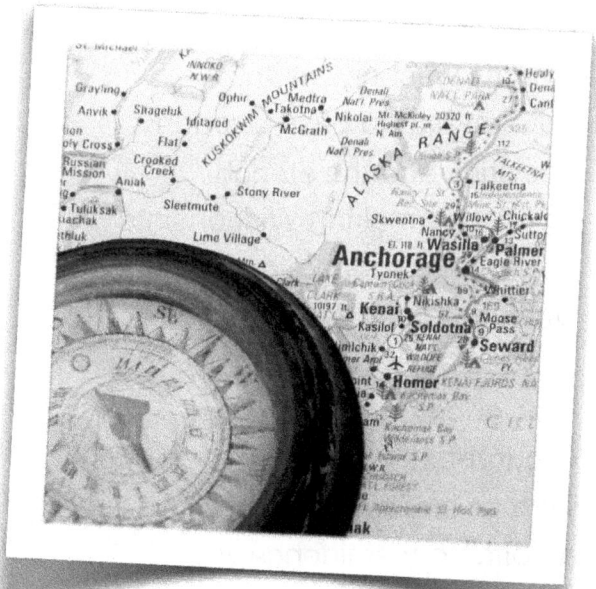

At 6 AM in the morning,
The day after our graduation,
The sun was happily irradiating,
Shimmering golden rays, emanating.

It was so beautifully adorning,
Marking our departure.
Acutely imbued with
Sentimental recollections,
And innumerable retrospections;
Fond childhood memories,
Of dearest Friends and Family.

We headed straight north,
For the bridge at Mackinaw,
Crossed over on into,
The frigid Upper Peninsula.

We took Highway 2,
Directly west to Duluth.
But first had to pass through
The stink and the stench,
Of cheese-making Wisconsin's
Voluminous mountains
Of algae-green excreta.

Icky, gooey, messy,
Ground-coating slushy,
With an aroma so pungent.
An olfactory eminence,
A robust, tangy fragrance,

That effluvial essence,
Of Guernsey-generating,
Bowel-moving emanations;
Methane gas redolence.

Most commonly known
To teary-eyed multitudes,
That plume of perfume,
Eternally emanating,
From bovine flatulence.
Gastric comestibles eradicating,
Copious colossal amounts,
Of their slippery poop,
Everywhere underfoot;
Plan ahead about wearing,
Your best rubber boots!

From Duluth to Grand Rapids to Bemidji;
To Grand Forks, North Dakota,
Devil's Lake, Minot, and Rugby.
The white owls were flying,
Six-foot wing spans just gliding,
Over the cornfields in the evening;
Extremely visually pleasing!
Hunting for field mice;
It was a beautiful sight.

Occasionally, just missing our camper,
They would give us a bit of a fright;
We still had quite a ways to go,
But had to keep driving real slow.

2 CANADA'S VAST REMOTE EXPANSE

We did not hit any low-flying owls
That flew down from the Polar Arctic;
A good omen on entering Canada,
This adventure had now really started.

Across the Canadian Border,
To Regina and Moose Jaw,
Onto Medicine Hat and Calgary;
Lots of prairie was all that we saw.

All of their AM radio stations
Just kept playing endlessly,
Over and over again, repetitiously
Bob Dylan's "Lay, Lady, Lay"
And Kenny Rodgers' "Ruuuuuby,
Don't Take Your Love To Town."
That DJ was some kind of clown!
The music deeply seated in our psyches,
Kept repeating over and over in our heads.

Our brains were swiftly becoming
A writhing and squirming, gelatinous mass.
Unfathomably, abysmally-imbedded,
Perpetually squiggling and wriggling,
Like crazed slimy worms jiggling,
Repetitiously twisting in our craniums;
We covered our ears from ultrasonic pain.

In the bright sunny morning,
Through the camper door opening,
We would watch prairie dogs cavorting;
Gathering food that they were hoarding.
On the prairie, so infinitely endless,
A vast landscape of dusty and brown,
Overflowing with hundreds of lakes,
Harboring disparate and distinct
Diversified Ganders and Drakes.

Multitudinous birds
Totaling into the thousands;
All manner of varied waterfowl
Abundantly proliferated,
Everywhere, all around.

Without wanting to stretch out the truth,
Possibly, I suspect maybe even,
They were numbering into the millions;
Everyone knew the real reason:
Because it was mating season!

Flying directly overhead in formations

In every possible direction all around,
The sky was alive, with rapid movement;
A cacophony, a chorus, of avian sound.

We were driving at night,
A ways north of Edmonton;
Two lanes running on each side,
With large islands in between.
When this immense, super-fast,
White, colossally-sized Wolf
Leapt right over the fence!
And in three hop, skip and jumps,
Crossed all the way over,
Leaped completely clean over,
The other 'bobwar' wire fence!
Incredibly, in a blink,
Disappeared into the trees,
That were impenetrably dense.

We were frozen in time,
For him to glide right on past,
Ten feet in front of our grille,
Just as if we were parked;
As if practically standing still.

While we had been truckin' along
At over 70 miles an hour,
He overwhelming displayed
Extreme power untamed;
Yet he barely had moved,
Like an ephemeral ghost.

He could travel at high speed,
Wherever choosing to go;
Swiftly, he dematerialized,
Right before our very eyes.

At Dawson Creek,
We reached the very beginning
Of the Alaska-Canada Highway;
Thirteen hundred miles unending,
A rocky, chuck-holed, dirt road.
Occasional trucks spreading gravel,
This road quickly makes tires unravel!
If you went any faster,
Than 30 miles an hour,
You would beat your truck to death;
Way out here, it would be a Disaster!

3 GROWLING GRIZZLY

Somewhere on the road, in between
Fort Nelson and Dawson Creek,
Driving north, bouncing crazily,
On the AL-CAN Highway all day,
We were abruptly amazed,
We could not help but to stare;
We were looking at a crazed Grizzly Bear.

The Bear was running parallel,
Like he had just recently escaped,
From a most-torturous Hell;
He was trapped, panicking, about to explode.

Along the left side of the road,
Larry pulled over to get a picture.
What we saw in this situation,
That had freaked out the Bear:
Five people were already working there.

With roaring lawnmowers and whining power trimmers,
The loud noises were frightening,
A frantic brown bear, seething and raging;
Most likely he had been peacefully sleeping,
Behind the tree line next to the cemetery.

They had aroused a sleeping Grizzly;
And he was running around crazy,
In a furious, hysterical, most-dangerous frenzy.

To that Bear, it must have been very scary;
Somehow he had entered this area errantly.
His progress was blocked by the superhighway;
Back and forth, up and down,
Near the side of the road, he was going insane,
Just trying to find a safe place to remain.

Larry took off with his camera;
I charged over to the landscapers.
I ran up and screamed,
"You'd better take cover, please,
There's a Bear going crazy,
On the other side of the trees!"

One man said, "Well, I'll be darned,
It has been quite a while."
He just stood there and smiled.
I could only shake my head,
I took off running again,
Back to where Larry
Was standing, looking down,
Into an opening in the hedge.

Larry was lining up his camera,
Just as I came running up there;
Also from the other direction,
So did that Gigantic Grizzly Bear!
The Bear hit the brakes and stood up,
Then he roared in our faces,
From only 12 feet away!

The camera went *click*,
And we took off running —
Lickety-split —
For the safety of our truck.
We then pulled it on up,
To the hedgerow tree line opening,
Where we could view
What we wanted to see;
Just what he was going to do.

That Bear was running,
Like a bat straight out of Hell,
In the *opposite* direction;
To who-knows-where? Oh well!
It seemed not to warrant,
Any serious attention,
From the workers previously mentioned,
So, amazed we got back on the road.

Apparently,
This wildlife episode
Was quite ordinary
To these Canadians,
If the truth be told.
Later we developed the picture;
Perfect from the waist up,
It clearly came out.
With raised giant paws,
His mouth roaring, wide open,
We were simple-mindedly lucky
That we didn't get mauled!

The place that turned out to be a highlight —
Liard Hot Springs Provincial Park;
We so badly needed a cleaning,
Our bodies were fetid and reeking.

From the bath shelter and stream,
We went and hiked up the path.
We found a 40-foot pond,
It was seven feet deep,
And it had its own wooden dock;
The water was refreshingly steaming hot.

We had stayed in for too long,
And when I got out,
The cold air briskly hit me,
I totally and immediately blacked out!

I hit the side of my face
On the edge of the dock;
Fell into the water face down;
But the warm temperature of the water
Was beginning to bring me around.

Suddenly Larry jumped in
And swiftly pulled my head out.
The blood and the cuts,
Scabbed up in my beard,
For the next couple of weeks;
It kept me looking so gruesomely weird.

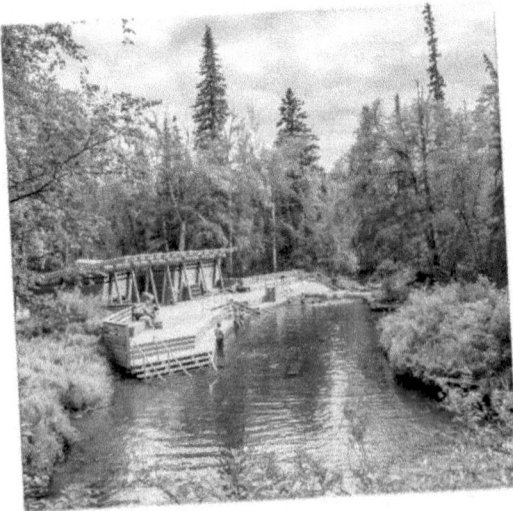

4 REQUIRED TO FIGHT WILDFIRE!

We were passing through forest fires,
Not too close, a few miles from the road.
We heard they were hiring firefighters,
For three dollars an hour, we were told.

But in Alaska, the 49th State,
More than double was the then-going rate.
Six dollars and fifty cents an hour,
Then they fly you in by helicopter.

After at least a week of firefighting,
They may bring you back down,
From that hot-burning mountain.
But if you just happen to die
It then saves them the time!

Personally
I had no desire
To be a heroic firefighter;
I did not, at all, aspire,
To quell any fire.
Had not the insanity,
That this onerous job would require.

As we drove on into Whitehorse Junction,
We were stopped by an erected roadblock
Of Royal Canadian Mounted Police
And The Canadian Forest Service,
Who were detaining and inducting

Single, physically-able young men;
Drafted into the Forest Service,
Onto their Firefighting Crews.
Our only other choice, if we fail,
Was to go to a Provincial Jail,
An alternative we would prefer not to do.

Forced to raise our right hands,
Swear allegiance to the Queen,
Totally against our American will
We mumbled and grumbled,
"Yes Sir, right on, Buffalo Bill!"
They then commanded,
These Dudleys, these Do-Righters,
"You will be on time reporting,
At 6 AM in the morning."
Zealously we responded,
"Oh, of course, we surely will!"

Again, mumbling under our breaths,
"We'll see you at dawn, Buffalo Bill."

We drove on up the hill,
Towards the back end of the town.
A beautiful view of the highway,
We could see quite aways, up and down.
Up to the bend, past the roadblock;
A very good view all around.
There was nothing really to stop us,
So we drove back on down
To the other side of the hill,
Where there were no Lawmen
Officially hanging around.

We got back on the road,
Noiselessly slipped out of town;
We kept on driving all night,
Being cautious, not wanting to be found.
We drove on through the night,
In the blue-gray setting light,
With thick forests overreaching,
On each side of the road.
Half a mile away in the mist,
Standing out there was a bridge,
Way out here with no reason to exist,
It did not quite make any sense.
In the twilight, straining visually,
We were squinting hard,
Just trying to see.
As we got closer,

We drove slower and slower;
About two blocks away we stopped,
Our jaws had completely dropped.
It was a gigantic, large Moose,
With his feet on each side of the road;
He was staring and glaring at us.

I turned off the engine,
We sat excitedly, very quietly,
For at least 15 minutes;
Undeniably, indescribably,
Spectacularly stunning!
Finally, he casually moseyed on,
Disdainfully looking down upon,
A couple of puny teenage kids;
Two tiny, hairless hominids.
We had no childish intention,
Of trying to get his attention.

5 SIRENIC HITCHHIKER

Somewhere near the Yukon Crossing,
We spotted a very attractive Blond.
She was backpacking a full load,
With her thumb sticking out.
Surrounded by dark wilderness,
With wild animals all about.
Unaided, companionless, all alone,
Not a soul to hear her shout;
She was casually hitchhiking,
Conspicuous on the side of the road.

Why, of course, we invited her, without delay!
We were recently just born yesterday.
We naively offered to pick her right up,
Because we had just recently fell,
Right off of the back of a Turnip Truck.

She was just heading on home,
To the quaint, little town of Mayo,
On the end of a dead-end road;
A secluded village,
Off of the highway.
What she didn't really want to tell us,
Was that it was a Government
Native Indian Settlement.
We were greeted
As soon as we arrived,
With long knives and accusations.
The girl had to convince them

That we had not tried to grab her ass.
Thankfully and luckily, once again,
We had been Perfect Gentlemen.

She emphatically convinced us
That we would be wise to stay
For a previously-promised dinner,
Of a sauce, quickly homemade.
It was really crappy spaghetti;
We really did not want to eat any,
But we finished it gracefully.

The young braves were whooping it up,
Dancing and running around with drums,
Half drunk and stumbling,
Hallucinating and bumbling,
Acting creepy and looking spacey;
We had to be very careful,
Not to offend anyone crazy!

As soon as we were done,
We told them we were On The Run
From the Royal Canadian Mounties;
They thought for a while and considered,
That it was all really excellent good fun!

As soon as we finished our dinner,
We gave thanks very sweetly,
And departed expeditiously,
Hastily, speedily, damned-fast, quickly!

6 GRAYLING WISHING WHILE FISHING

Moving on to Dawson,
We stopped at a campground
On the river called the Yukon.
We discovered a gaggle of fisherman,
All chatting and casting,
Unsuccessfully catching,
A truly empirical fish:
The exquisitely, elegant Grayling;
Delicious on anyone's white dish.
On the Au Sable River in Michigan,
They had gone completely extinct,
Back in1926.
This delicate, most-sensitive fish,
Was unable to tolerate
Any kind of pollution;
Extermination was the sad resolution.

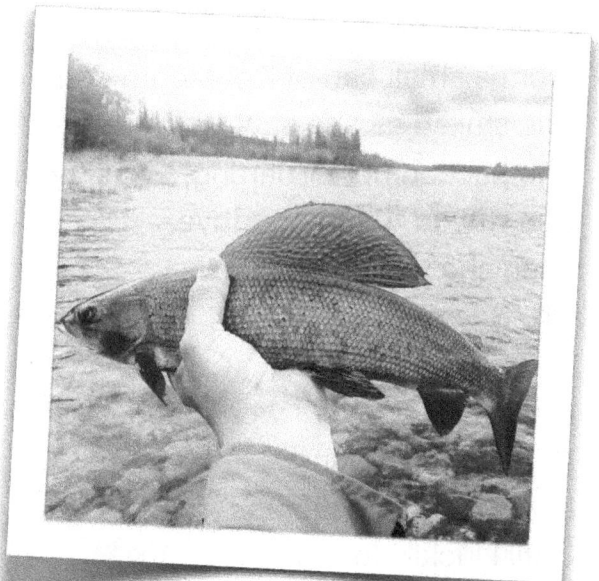

One of the older fishermen,
Had caught two, using artificial lures;
That was the total of all that was caught,
By fifteen fishing lines, all for naught!

I looked way up the river,
And saw in the distance
A standing alone figure,
Lazily pitching proficient.

Casually casting my line,
Inauspiciously taking my time,
Working my way by the bye,
To my delightful surprise,
What did I agreeably find?
An attractive, Indian woman, thirtyish;
And she had a very long string of fish!

I watched as she baited her hook,
From a small can of Del Monte corn.
She smiled as she saw me taking a look,
She packed up, departing; I was forlorn.
She waved to me goodbye,
Then she went on her way.
Oh, what a beautiful day!

In waders, upriver I went back,
Rummaged around
In the camper's storage rack.
Until I luckily found,
A can that was precious;

Kernels of corn, so delicious,
To those most-extremely, picky fish!

I was now devising my plan,
Calculating it all in my head.
How I was going to tell Larry
About the bait, very surreptitiously;
Avoiding other fishermen especially!

Everyone else in the campground
Was heading back indoors,
Getting ready for bed.
This was my chance to be slick,
Finally for a change.
It was going to be my turn,
To show the experienced Larry,
My new Northwest Territories-
Native American-
Outdoorsman trick.

The sun had descended,
One-third of the way down,
Then it slowly shifted to the right.
Then just around midnight,
It was on the horizon,
Shining directly due North.
It was our first time to witness,
The brilliance and brightness,
Of the perpetual Midnight Sun.

At 3 AM in the morning,
The full circle was forming.
Majestically, it started rising,
Ascending above,
The eastern horizon.

By this time
We had counted
As many Grayling
As we had fingers;
That is how many
We had on our stringer!

We cleaned up the fish,
And we fried up our breakfast;
With onions and potatoes,
It was especially succulent.

As the other campers awoke,
We offered them up
The rest of our catch;
To all of those folks,
That expressed such a wish,
To share all of our fish.
I was so proud of myself,
I felt so accomplished!

7 APPRAISING ANCHORAGE

Moving on forward to Little Gold,
Across the International Border,
There was little to be told.
Pushing on to Tok Junction,
Kept driving on to Glennallen,
Finding safe passage,
Driving down to Anchorage.

We were touring Anchorage lazily,
Then we went on down to the sea,
To view the wrinkled ground,
Where a major earthquake did abound;
It looked like the wrinkled folds in the face
Of a Chinese dog called the Shar-Pei.
Where Mother Nature
Had lain down her Mark;
Five foot-high ridges of dirt
Were turned into a Memorial Park.

Dedicated to all of the Good Citizens,
Their friends and their family,
And any of their kin,
Who had tragically been killed,
Disappeared or gone missing;
During the Alaska Earthquake,
There were many it did take!

In 1964,
On March 27th, Good Friday,
At 5:36 PM, people were having their dinner,
Returning from church,
Or from work, coming home.
Life as everyone had known,
Would not exist anymore;
It disappeared in a few minutes
Their world had gone out of control.

Alaska's one-and-only city
Now was looking shiny and new,
It was looking fairly modern;
I was seeing opportunity here.

But Larry really didn't discern;
He had no interest in living there.
He was contemplating
Something much more rustic.
He wanted to head on back,
All the way northeast to Tok Junction.
From there we caught the road going south,
To Haines, on the Inside Passage, at its mouth.

We slept near the water,
Inside of an old, weathered cabin,
With the names and the years,
Of previous gold seekers,
Carved historically into the walls.
Gold Rushers 70 years ago
Started their long trek
Right exactly from here.
Here was their last epitaph;
There would be no gravestones.
Where these Cheechakos were going,
Many would die, without finding their gold.
Dates going all the way back to 1901,
That is what those Victorian carvings told.

We went and sat by the shore,
Observing the frolicking seals.
This was the first time I saw orcas,

With their exhorting squeals full of zeal.
They came so incredibly close,
Who was by who, being more observed?
We were somewhat uncomfortably unsure!

We jumped in to go swimming,
We could barely breathe to crawl out;
Immediately we were becoming,
Flash-frozen like vegetable sprouts!

Our legs hastily were benumbing,
Our body temperatures rapidly plunging,
To exposure, we were quickly succumbing,
Even with determined resolution,
We were barely able to dog-paddle in!

Brought down to our hands and knees,
We were scarcely able to grovel out,
Exhausted, we promptly collapsed,
Fully debilitated, prostrated;
All of our energy was sapped.

After recovering from our freezing, frigid bath,
We went to Haines and boarded the car ferry;
Onto Juneau, our final destination, at last!

Just off of the highway we briskly had traveled,
Another panoramic 600 miles;
Navigating our way from Anchorage
Through the most magnificent,
Supremely exquisite, forested wilds.

266

The truck was still performing without fault,
On Alaska's fresh and well-maintained asphalt.

But yet again,
Larry had been very adamant;
My wish to stay in Anchorage,
He was having none of it.
I thought, "Oh Hell,
I might as well
See all of it."
But I was beginning to realize,
That this partnership,
Was not going to survive.

8 GETTING TO KNOW JUNEAU

We arrived in Juneau,
And Larry was a happy guy.
We found a cabin,
Out by the glacier,
Where the cold winds blow,
On Mendenhall Loop Road.
We tar papered the roof,
And installed a wood stove.
We had gotten permission,
From a wealthy investor,
And the rent was free — very cool! —
As long as we registered to enter school.
We were accepted at Mendenhall Junior College;
Roofing and a wood stove was all we had to do!

We met these two construction guys,
That had a government landscaping contract
To seed grass on 30 miles of the Juneau Highway;
And they needed to hire two guys right away.

In order to hire laborers,
There was a Union Waiting List.
So instead, we planned to register,
As Landscape Engineers.
We said our age was eighteen;
They believed us without any ID!
In walked the two construction guys,
Who came there looking to hire
Specifically "Two Landscape Engineers."

The clerk said, "We have what you desire,
What an amazing coincidence!"
She looked like a Norman Rockwell painting,
Of such lovely, trusting innocence!
I still wonder to this very day,
If she ever figured out the gist,
Or if it ever dawned on her,
About exactly what she had missed?

The dirt next to the highway
Originated from the seashore.
Because it was all full of salt,
It had to be balanced with lime,
A chemical that is very alkaline.

Our job was to go everywhere
That the landscaping machine didn't dare.
They gave us a pick-up truck,
Two wheelbarrows, shovels and rakes.
Backing up to a semi-trailer truck,
We began to unload
One-hundred-pound bags of lime.
Irritating our eyes, all of the time,
Inhaled into our noses,
And getting into our cuts,
Searing under our fingernails,
Mixed in with the grime;
Burning continuously,
All of the time!
When we got off of work,

Our backs were bent over;
But they paid us eight-fifty an hour!
Much better than six, fighting a forest fire.

Still to this day, where we had spread caustic lime,
Up on the hillside, on a new road freshly driven,
There lies the very greenest of grass,
On Alaska's State Highway Number Seven,
Because we faithfully Busted Our Ass!

We also went fishing and hiking,
We did plenty enough of that,
But everything was done soaking wet.
The drizzling precipitation every day,
All day long, throughout the summer;
The showers were a continual bummer!

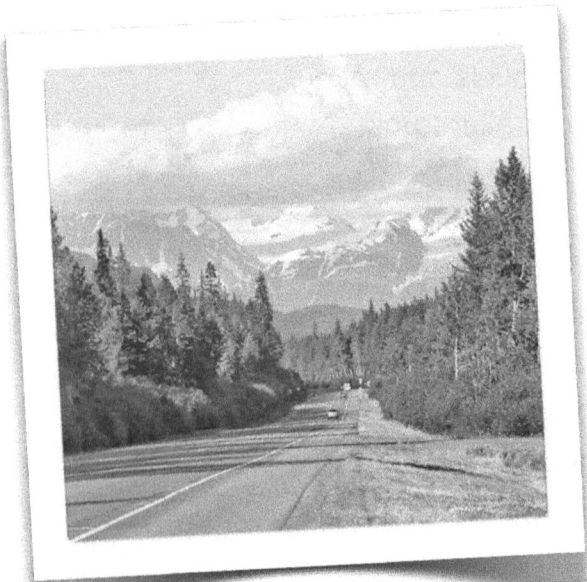

9 PEACEFULLY PARTING WAYS

For me,
It was getting to be,
About my time to leave,
Literally!
I was going to tell Larry,
That this just wasn't me;
I was going to California
To get some sunshine,
And be surrounded by almonds,
Orange trees, and grapevines.
Hoping to meet,
A few California Girls;
Have a few whirls, dance a few twirls,
Maybe some romance,
Maybe some birds and some bees.
A California Community College,
Most unequivocally,
Was seductively calling to me,
Like Nordic Sirens of the Sea.

In those days in California,
The first two years
Of college tuition was free.
The only expense was the books,
And the thirty-five dollar
Student registration fee.

So Larry and I went down to the car dealer,
And traded in our camper pick-up truck

For a beat-up Plymouth Valiant,
And also three hundred bucks.

I got the money,
Larry got the car.
I bought a plane ticket
For a San-Francisco-Fresh-Start.

I arrived at the San Fran airport
Fairly late, around midnight;
Not a single bus or taxi in sight.
When I met this elderly man,
Jauntily wearing a chauffeur's cap.
His reservation had fallen through,
He said he would take me to
My sister's house,
In the middle of the city,
In his beautiful, black,
Limousine Cadillac.
I could arrive and impress,
Looking like a Major Success!

He would be more than happy
To drop me off for only ten bucks.
I was having an exceptional day;
I was surely having marvelous good luck!

I arrived very late,
Woke up my Sister and Brother-in-Law;
I'd shown up without warning,
I had not even called.

Here I was,
In the very early morning,
About one thirty AM,
My first time in San Fran.

It was the late summer of '69,
On my 18th birthday,
I was so looking forward,
To an Excellent, Good-Time Stay!

LOTTERY DRAFT

1 SIGNED, SEALED AND DELIVERED

Back in 1970 during the Vietnam War,

America had a strict policy called the Draft.

Where suddenly a young man might lose his craft;

His future (and possibly his life) was hijacked.

The Government seemed to think

That they owned us - blood and soul.

To use us like cotton-picking slaves,

Sending teenage boys to their graves,

For their accidental illegal warfare,

A war that had been falsely declared.

The imbroglio in the Bay of Tonkin was bad,

The USS Maddox's now false claim of attack

By North Vietnamese torpedoes was totally false;

It was only one single bullet hole found in a bulkhead,

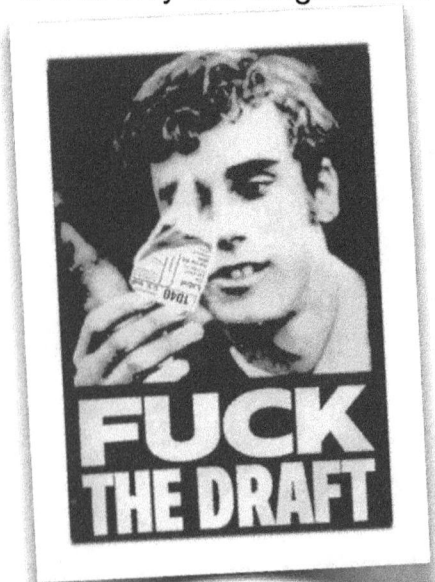

But the President and his advisors were at a loss,
For multiple reasons they had to lie to Congress,
To support their expansion of the War at all costs.

The U.S. detected three Ghostly torpedoes,
The purported torpedo attack on the USS Maddox,
Turned out to be one bullet hole from a single rifle.
This Vietnam War was begun on a Radar mistake,
To propagate illegal warfare, the media was stifled.

This was their opportunity to use
Leftover ordnance and C-rations;
So much decades-old, expired canned food,
That was left over from World War II.
During that War we promised Ho Chi Minh,
That if he helped us fight the Japanese,
Instead of returning Vietnam back to France,
We would make it democratically free.
But we lied, and after the War had passed,
We reinstituted it right back to France.

Back in the 1950s we sent in advisors
To fight Ho Chi Minh, our old ally,
Because he was inheriting
Free munitions from Russia and China.
So now America divided their land,
Into a North and South Vietnam.
We sent in thousands, like ants,
Of our 18-year old male children,
To be slaughtered just like cattle
Trapped inside a rendering plant.

Eight weeks of Basic Training
Does not prepare anyone
For sophisticated jungle warfare,
Hand-to-hand combat, or bombs.
The military had thought,
That watching the war on TV,
Would make us all inspired;
Our militancy was desired.
Instead we witnessed our children
Being shot full of holes,
And being blown to pieces,
For what, nobody knows.
It was all one big sick, fucking joke!

The Government ran
This Draft Board Campaign Of Fear,
And they were shipping boys off,
From the ones they held dear.

But if one could afford to go to college,
Then they could have their induction deferred.
This was okay for those Wealthy Sons,
But not so well for the Poor Son Of A Guns,
Or the young working stiffs,
Just trying to make it alone.
It pretty much took all of their hope,
When everything was all said and done.

They were forced to submit
To Modern Global Warfare,
Or just keep running scared
From an illegal Draft Board
Carried over from a World War II Accord.
If you got stopped by the cops,
For anything petty that was charged,
The first thing they demanded to see
Was your Selective Service Card.

If you did not possess one,
You automatically went to jail.
Some guys got so scared,
They went and volunteered
For a mud-soaked Living Hell.
And instead of only two years,
They signed up for three or four.
Some got talked into even more,
Thinking they would get
Special favorable treatment,
Somewhere else, other than the war.
But unless you managed to get,

Extremely-high test scores,
On the Military's Multiple Choice Test,
You were going to spend,
All of your time in the end,
In muddy rice paddies,
Or under mountaintop canopies.
And when they gave you a little time off,
You would be spending your money in scores,
Escaping your fate, drowning your sorrows,
In alcohol, along with the Vietnamese whores.

Hope of our Heroes returning increases,
But I had friends who would never come back,
Although some did come home in broken pieces
In nondescript zippered black plastic sacks.

That is when I decided I was going to try,
And fight against this conscription.

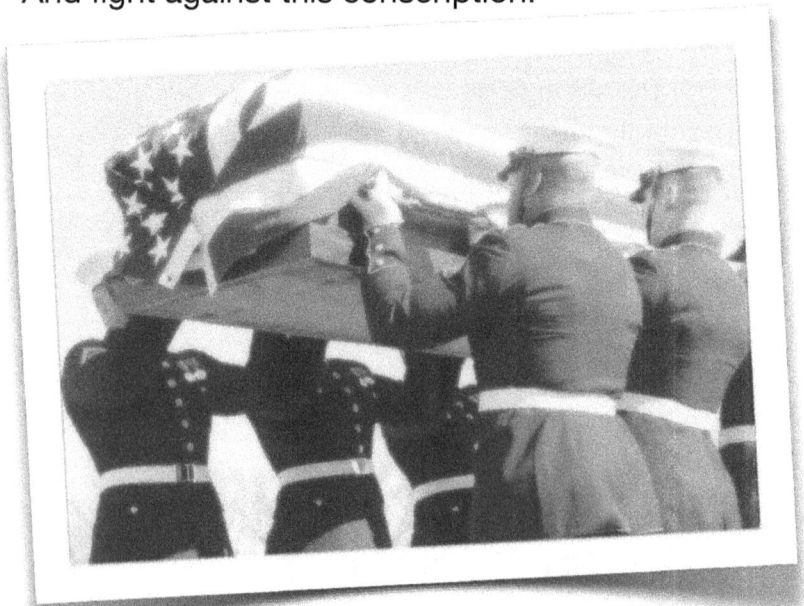

My freedom was being attacked,
I was going to dodge this induction!

I had already turned down
A generous nomination to West Point,
From our Congressman in Michigan;
Supposedly four years of free college!
But the Harsh Reality,
Of this prestigious education,
Was that after just one year of college,
I would be quickly moving on,
To the lush, verdant, tropical gardens,
Converted into a rotting, war-infested,
Prodigiously sexually-infected,
Now inelegant Republic of South Vietnam.

It was common to be shot
By your own men not very long after
The first time you were dropped
From the U.S. Cavalry helicopter.
With your Infantrymen all jingoistic
And no spare time to abide any fools,
A friendly .223 caliber bullet,
Sooner than later might get you popped.

My Father was furiously incensed
That I had so readily turned down,
Such a lucrative and appealing offer,
From President Lyndon B. Johnson.
My Father refused
To ever speak to me again.

So our dinners were silent,
Till I graduated high school,
And I went out on the road again.

I left home for good,
And for the next 20 years,
I never spoke to him again;
Neither of us shed any tears.

He was completely brainwashed
By the United States Military.
Because of his training, he totally believed
That the experience of Military Service
For maturement, was just the greatest thing.
Greater than the invention of sliced bread.
He had always insisted that Nixon should be King!

When my Dad heard I was working
In San Francisco for the Phone Company,
Instead of off fighting in Vietnam,
He decided he was going to narc on me;
Rat me out to the Draft Board anonymously.

Why should I risk my only young life,
To make that misguided man proud of me?
My Mother stood up for me and told him
"If you forsake your own Son
To the Military Draft
Then I am all through
With your sorry ass."
(Huge kudos to Mom!)
280

I would make my deliveries
To the Phone Company buildings.
From many floors up above,
I could see so very clearly.
I would observe distinctly below,
People with signs on the sidewalks;
At 'The Bank of Hysteria's' massive front doors.
They were young men, women and children,
Who were just peacefully protesting the war.

The Bankers must have never heard
Of America's Bill of Rights.
So instead of letting the people protest—
Just let it run out its natural course—
The Financiers would call out the Cops,
Who would smash, bash and crash,
With their big, heavy horses,
And their Harley-Davidson motorcycles.

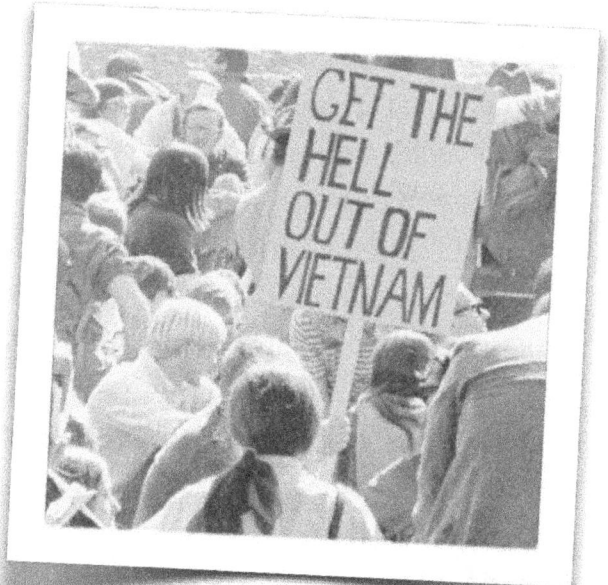

The Bluecoats drove onto the crowded sidewalks
With sadistic, careless abandon,
Into the young women and children;
I was mortified as a human!

The Dissenters were just enthusiastically walking,
Holding up their homemade signs;
Peacefully protesting on the sidewalk.
Just demonstrating and exercising,
What used to be their Civil Rights.
Guaranteed, by the U.S.Constitution.
Has anyone heard of that institution?

I do not care that you would dare,
Without any first-hand knowledge,
To object and call me a liar.
But I personally witnessed it.
And it was all very disgusting;
I could only shake my head.
This is when I started realizing,
That corrupt Corporate Bankers
Were virtually capitalizing
On the sacrifices of the Dead!
How much my country had changed,
What it was now really all about.
No longer was it what they had taught us
In Government Civics class,
What we for so long had believed in,
It no longer was around!

Nowadays, even Political Science

No longer is part of the curriculum.
Do you think that was just an accident?
Because Rockefeller Inc. owned the only four
Public School educational publishing companies,
Teaching Government in public school
Has ceased and is publicly deceased!
And only idiots are foolish enough to believe,
That it was all just a coincidence of budgeting needs.

The fiends who were really in charge,
Were the War Machine Industrial Complex;
They were making money Hand Over Fist!
The Rockefellers also owned the Colt factory in Texas,
Where The Family was mass producing
The new .223-caliber AR-15s,
Plus all of the Military's large weaponry.
What the Rockefeller Family also owned,
Was a Czechoslovakian factory,
Where the Communist's AK-47s
Were mass produced, and manufactured,
Plus most of their other heavy ordnance.
These were made within accordance,
Of World War I's Geneva Concordance
To supply all of the world's Communists.
Then they gave one to every soldier,
In every radical country that was pissed!

The evil that you will soon discover and abhor,
Was that they were making all of the weaponry,
For both sides of this loathsome, hideous war!
It was one great, giant, hopped-up travesty,

A Steroid Satanic Insane Fantasy.

The Military Industrial Complex,
Keeps on perpetuating itself;
That is its primary intent.
They had to cover up the shouts;
What in the Hell was really going on?
Extending European Colonization,
That is what it was really all about!

Watching every evening on television
Hideous war-wound traumatization;
It was an Apocalypse we were witnessing,
A compelling, most-terrifying conflagration!

So they could malevolently maintain,
A never-ending financial drain.
The Irony and Total Injustice of it all,
Was that you could go and die for your country,

But you couldn't vote or even drink alcohol!

Watching the Police viciously attack
Helpless Hippie men, women and children,
Who had the nerve to be so boldly audacious
As to clean up all of the rubbish and trash
On a municipal, abandoned, dirt parking lot;
The idea was so completely outrageous!

The people, of their own volition,
Planted bushes and trees and grass,
On this unused vacant lot in Berkeley.
Turned it into a free public space,
They appropriately named it People's Park.

How could the City Administration
Act out so bizarrely and bezerkely?
Attacking, bulldozing and bludgeoning,
Clubbing, abusing and bruising,
Spraying tear gas everywhere,
While the children's eyes were burning!

One of my co-workers,
Was merely just leaning
Against a city-street signpost,
When this Keystone Cop came running
Up the street from behind;
He saw my guy standing there, observing,
From across the street, kitty-corner.
Curiously studying, just trying to see.
He was an on-the-clock employee,

My co-worker and friend,
A Phone Company Driver of PT&T.

The Cop had his shotgun, just looking for fun,
He was feeling so much joy and jubilation,
Then, without warning, and no hesitation,
Shot my co-worker in the backside with buckshot.
He spent three weeks on his stomach in the hospital;
From his serious wounds, he had to convalesce a lot.

I don't care what you say -
I know that a lot of Cops are corrupt;
Some incompetent, many inept.
You can believe what you want,
But this blitzkrieg on the public was a fact,
And that is about all
That I have to say about that.

I came home from work
Shocked to find that my roommate was out;
He'd been busted, was what our neighbor had told me.
Six gruff, hostile, draft-dodger-searching FBI men
Had handcuffed and arrested him,
Then they dragged him downtown.
Just like that, so matter of fact, such total nonsense.
When pseudo-Nazis come to your residence,
Forcibly kick or force your door open,
They don't mess around, just break it right down.
As I was pondering all of my options,
I was contemplating what next I should do,
When my roommate showed up at the door
286

And he said "Dude, how do you do?"
That is when my jaw hit the floor!

I said,"What is the Deal with you,
Busted for not showing up for your physical.
How come you are not sad and blue?"
He said,"One call to my lawyer,
Then in just two hours I was let loose."
I said,"Well, that's a Hell of a good thing;
I want to retain that lawyer too."

That is when I promised myself
That I would refuse submitting.
Unless they were very willing
To strong-arm me all of the way,
To give me some serious jail time abuse.
Otherwise I was just going to stay out on the loose.

2 INDUCTION INSTRUCTION

I told my story to another co-worker,
This very-good-looking,
Hollywood-blond surfer guy.
Since he was already married,
When he was finally drafted,
They gave him the option to volunteer
For some easy radio duty in Hawai'i.
He was now going to be surfing all day,
Laying on the beach, drinking Primo beer!

I mentioned to him that I must report soon
For my military induction physical,
And he said,"Have I got a story for you!"

"When I went across the Bay
To the Oakland Induction Center,
They gave me all of my medical test papers.

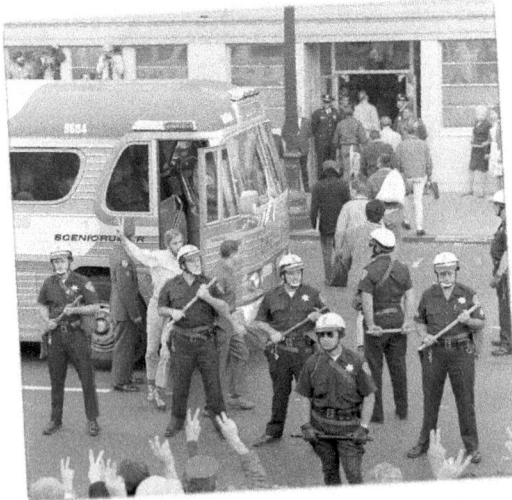

And instead of standing in line,
I went and snuck out the door!
No one contacted me,
For over a year.
It was at the LA Induction Center,
Where I had originally registered,
That they managed to discover the discrepancy,
Then they notified Oakland to find out
Why I had not yet entered the Military.
That is who brought it
To Oakland's attention.
Otherwise, I believe,
That this inconsistency
Would have never been detected."

I said,"Oh Hell, yes,
I am going to give it a go!"
So that's what I did.
I dutifully followed his directions,
And all of the different colored lines,
All the way on up to the third floor;
I gave them some of the paperwork
For a chest X-ray and blood work.

Next I was going to have to
Get undressed and give up my clothes;
Stand in a line and bend over,
Spreading my cheeks like a Punk,
So some underpaid Army Doctor
Could have a long look up my butt.
This was my chance!

I ducked into a stairwell,
Put back on my shirt,
And stuffed all of the rest
Of my stack of paperwork
Down the front of my pants.

Down the stairs I danced,
I came out on the second floor,
And marched towards the back.
(I accidentally walked right through
A meeting of military officers,
But my mission was still intact!)
I spotted a service elevator
And reached for the button,
Acting nonchalantly, just like
I was a delivery guy on the run.

I got on the elevator,
Rode down to the first floor; lo and behold,
There sitting and reading at his desk,
Was a private Security Guard, all alone.
Hitting the crossbar on the back door,
I walked unhurriedly and most deliberately,
Stepping out into the bright sunlight once more.
I then walked along under the freeway,
Till I came to an on-ramp, heading west,
And gleefully and conspiratorially,
Bravely and excitedly,
I stuck out my thumb,
Defiantly and courageously,
In front of a few indifferent bums.

It wasn't very long
Before a black guy picked me up.
He had such a huge smile,
And he told me
That he worked for
The Anti-War Coalition
At San Jose State,
And that he was a bright academician,
On a full scholarship.

After hearing about that,
I couldn't help telling him
Exactly what I had just done.
He said "You were great! `
Let me tell you how *I* had my fun."

"You know those yellow-
Red- green- and blue-colored lines,
That they make you follow
Every time, for your physical test?
Well, I kept on acting confused,
Carefully always making sure,
To end up in the wrong line.
And after two days, they told me
"Go on home, Nigger,
You're just too damned dumb
To be a member
Of the American Military."

I found this rendition of his story
To be promptly and summarily,

Full of happy, heartening hilarity!

He kindly went out of his way,
And dropped me off across the Bay,
At the San Francisco bus station downtown.
We traded motivational slogans,
We were jiving, getting on down;
There was cheerful well-wishing all around.
We shook hands and high fived our goodbyes.
Then I caught a streetcar to Twin Peaks,
Where I lived in the middle of this Hippie town.
To me, he was a very good Brother,
I experienced a newfound respect,
Which had developed during this ride,
A more open-mind toward all Brothers,
Since having just encountered each other.

3 INDUCTION RESUMPTION

A year had gone by
Until I was called to come back.
The two documents I had left,
Had made me too easy to track.

By standing in all of the wrong lines,
I managed to drag it out another day.
For those that didn't finish their physical,
They were required to stay another day.

They put us up at a decent hotel,
Close by the Induction Center;
A gay, No-Tell Hotel,
At your own risk, you enter!
I got to know a few of the guys,
And they wanted me to join them
To go beat up this queer;
Wanting to take all of his money.

This very-good-looking guy in a suit,
Had parked right out front of the Center,
He was standing next to his tan Jaguar,
He was making goo-goo eyes at the guys;
He wanted them to grab a cab,
And follow his beautiful new car
Right on down to the beach.
I knew he had a lesson to teach.

I said, "No thank you, guys.

That is not very wise,
And it is not very kind.
And besides,
He might have a surprise,
A certain reprise,
Cause you deep pain of some kind;
It might very well be your demise."

Sure enough,
When he was surrounded by the six guys,
He said, "There is nothing
That I like more than queering,
Except freestyle street-fighting;
You boys will be such a delight!"

Those six guys went to the hospital
With lots of bruises and contusions.
I joined the other crowd that was toking;
A bag of weed they were rolling and smoking.
And after about an hour of taking tokes,
Of blowing lots of marijuana smoke
In one of the rooms, we had developed
A giant, humongous thirst for some beer.

The guys all delegated me;
I was elected to attempt to buy beer,
Since they said I looked like the oldest.
I had a few whiskers on my chin;
Even though I was still pretty thin,
I was certainly willing to give it a spin.

294

One 17-year-old country boy,
Just a poor, teat-pulling, cow-milker,
Had put up most of the money.
He said that what he really wanted
Was to get stinking drunk today.
Because he had gotten caught
In a barn, in the hay,
With a 15-year-old girl;
It definitely wasn't his day.
His trial Judge came from Hell;
Not content with just ruining his life,
He wanted this young,
Seventeen-year-old lad
As a human sacrifice!
The Judge, of course, then told him his plan.
"Either you are going to go to prison,
Or imagine this sparkling clear vision:
You can take a government vacation,
To a tropical resort, a Vietnam destination."

It was just a little after dark,
We hit the funky streets on a lark,
In deserted, destitute, downtown Oakland;
Looking for some beer was the plan.
We found a mom-and-pop Asian grocery store.
As I mustered up all of my confidence,
Self-assuredly I walked through their front door.

Thinking they might be impressed,
With seeing my few scrawny whiskers,
For ID, I was hoping they wouldn't ask.
I bought two-and-a-half cases
Of 16-ounce Colt 45;
We were not planning to drive!
The seven of us
All marched back into the hotel;
One of us was carrying the prize.
We all got into the elevator,
Then the door closed, shut tight.

A split-second later
Just before we head up
We heard a bell ding
And the door opened back up.

A pompous Marine Sergeant,
In his olive dress uniform,
Charged in and said,
"Hear, hear, hear, I fear,
I am sorry to inform you, but
I am confiscating this beer."
296

I protested, "You cannot do that,
We are in a public hotel!"
He said, "Go ahead, and go tell.
The government has leased it,
So now this is government property;
Everywhere on these premises,
Alcohol is not permissible!"

The gay bellboys readily
Grabbed all of our beer;
A confiscation corruption!
They whisked away all of our brew,
Through a lobby door, into a back room,
For their subsequent, private consumption,
It was more than obvious to assume.
Pointing, he said,
"All of you guys
Come on over here,

Get out your IDs,
Put them on my desk,
Exactly right there."

I was the only guy
That didn't have an ID;
Those dummies had all volunteered.
They were all going to be Grunts,
They had all gotten a bum steer!

I had to ask,
"What is your plan?
What are you going to do,
With all of those IDs?"
He said,
"You are all going to do some Brig Time,
Before you start your Basic Training;
You guys really fucked up this time!"

So that's when I hit him;
Jammed my left forearm
Right on into his throat.
Smashed him backwards into the wall,
With his feet dangling off of the floor.

I yelled to the awe-struck queers,
"You had better move fast,
You had better go get me my beer.
Because this highfalutin asshole,
That you hold so dear,
Will be waiting for you
Just like Art on the wall,
Trying hard to suck air."

I told all of the guys,
"Grab your IDs,
Right now we are getting
The Hell out of here!"
I warned the Marine Sergeant,
"You'd better not call the Cops,
Or I may have business to do,
Coming back here just for you!"

I knew I was bluffing—
A little huffing and puffing—
But it gave him an authentically-good scare;
And then I messed up his hair!
We stormed right on out
Through the glass doors out in front,
Into the bright starry light.

We were going to party all night.
We were going to get really tight!

I led them into the back alleys
Of Oakland's grimy Downtown,
And I said, "I have to confide,
That we swiftly must hide;
Soon the Cops will be coming around!"

We managed to find
A shadowy stairwell in the dark,
Plenty of room to relax on the stairs,
While throwing down a few beers.
Passing around some more reefers
To park and spark in the dark,
And possibly meditate and think,
On how swiftly things change,
In a cosmic, split-second blink!

"Hey everyone, shut up and be quiet!"
Sure enough, just as soon as I said it,
Guess who decides to come driving by?
But an Oakland Police cruiser,
With its police radio blasting on high,
Shining their bright spotlights
All over the back alley walls.

I said to the guys, "Just try to be cool,
These Cops won't be leaving their cars;
They know this is a dangerous neighborhood,
And they definitely are not,

Going to be acting like fools."
They drove right on by
And they left us all alone,
To consume two-and-a-half cases
Of high-alcoholic-content Colt 45;
We just kept right on drinking,
Until all of the malt liquor was gone.

By the time we had finished
We were pretty badly messed up,
Staggering blindly around,
In a spinning dark cloud,
All over the alley, throwing up.
I was now starting to realize,
That I had not properly analyzed,
I had not quite thought this thing through.
I just wanted to go rest my head,
On that soft hotel bed.

I was pretty sure
That I was going to Jail.
And I thought that this party,
Would soon fall off of the rails.
This just might be a good time,
To confront my personal problems,
With the Agency of Selective Service Slavers,
To get myself completely rejected forever!

The next morning
I woke up
To a banging in my head,

And a banging on the door.
And so innocently I said, "Yes?"
They loudly answered
"Mr. Fotherby, you can get dressed;
It is time for you to leave."

It was only 7 AM, and I thought,
"Oh what the Hell,
I am going off to Jail."
I quickly got dressed,
Unleveled, disheveled,
My hair was a mess,
A little stinky, at best.

Stepped into the hallway,
Next to my Military Guide,
Off to the lobby I was led
To take my Jailhouse Ride.

At the door stood a gauntlet
Of 12 stocky Marines,
In dress uniforms,
With fixed bayonets,
On their bolt-action rifles.
What they had in store for me,
I had no clue as of yet.

I looked at my Guide and I said,
"What the Fuck, are you kidding me?"
He said, "Listen up, Mr. Fotherby,
This is the news:

302

You had better wise up very soon.
Now get the Hell out of here!"

I daintily danced, and happily pranced,
My way in between,
Two rows of Marines
Standing at attention.
As I slid my way out through the door,
I could hardly believe,
My fortuitous, awesome dumb luck!
This was an incredible triumph
That I had just managed to duck.
Now I can see,
God was clearly
Looking out for me!

Again, I hiked on down to the on-ramp,
And joyously put out my thumb;
Back to San Francisco,
Where I was now from.

As soon as I returned home,
I immediately went to the fireplace,
And burned all of my draft papers,
Stirred the ashes and left not a trace.
Thinking, that had all been too easy,
For the assault that I had done.
I just kept on eerily thinking,
That there was a Black Cloud yet to come.

Eventually the Selective Service
Sent me my 1A Draft Card.
Then, they sent me another one.
And then, they sent me another one!

Curiously enough,
They never sent me a letter,
Nor any of my induction papers.
Which only left me to presume -
They would only have me assume -
That because I was somewhat incorrigible,
And I didn't really give a hot damn,
They must have thought that I was too violent,
Unfit for export to South Vietnam!

GOING DOWN TO MEXICO

1 EXCURSION

It was my College Spring Break in 1973,
I was starting to get apathetic and tired,
Of way too much tournament-fighting Karate.
I had my Toyota Corona five speed,
And about $200 in cash;
I figured that was about all that I'd need.

I thought I could make a quick dash,
Spend a week walking on the beach,
Down south on the West Coast in Guaymas.
I was dreaming of a vacation fantasy!
I just picked out a spot on the map;
I had nine days to get there and back.
Changed the oil, and got the car gassed;
Spring break was finally here at last.

From Santa Rosa, California,
I drove for two days without sleep.
Friends had given me a few warnings,
But I had not listened or paid any heed.

My engine was perfectly running,
I crossed the border at Calexico,
The economic decline was stunning.
Entering into Mexicali, Mexico,
I made sure to buy their insurance.
It was called Seguros Tepeyac S.A.,

A Mexican-brand insurance,
An important, stay-out-of-jail deterrent,
An escape from local Law Enforcement;
So that in the case of an accident,
I could still return home some day.

I then closely followed
Federale Autovia Numero Dos
All the way to Sonoyta, Sonora,
Then on to the beaches of Guaymas.
Just off of the highway a store was there
As I turned right, just heading on south,
I stopped and I bought a six-pack of beer,
To slake the thirst in my throat and my mouth.

Started driving on through
Ranchero-type country.

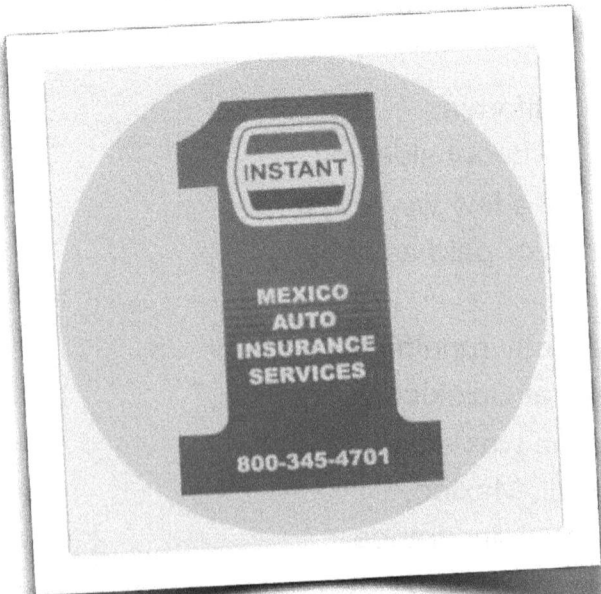

INSTANT

MEXICO
AUTO
INSURANCE
SERVICES

800-345-4701

I was just enjoying the view,
But I was beginning to get hungry.

Saw a vaquero hitchhiking,
A lonely cowboy by the side of the road,
To his strange face I took a liking.
As to understanding each other's language,
There was very much that we didn't know.

I stopped and picked him up,
And I offered him a beer,
But there was very little we could discuss,
If he knew of any hazards to fear.

No Policía were observed to be lurking;
I dropped him off a few miles down the road,
At the ranch where he had a job working.
Then I just kept on going
Off to the destination that I had chosen.

Heading deep out into the desert,
I drove through an ancient flood plain
Where the road had been built
On top of a 30-foot-high rock levee,
To protect it from spring-time runoff;
It was a desert highway on stilts.

With no shoulder on the side of the road.
I was starting to get tired, nodding, almost dozing.
There was nowhere to pull off,
My eyelids were becoming very heavy;

I intermittently began blacking out.
Those two beers were hitting me now -
I could no longer fend off the sleep -
And then I just abruptly passed out!

How far that I traveled,
Was just strictly dumb luck;
I was going minimally,
75 miles an hour.
I awoke and looked up,
When I heard a loud clunk,
As I flew off of the embankment,
At so very close to full power.

Ineffectually steering the wheel,
While flying through the air,
As my car from the skies descended,
This ride was quickly becoming,
Rather quite a bit of a scare.
Attempting to fight off
An overwhelming panic,
In a gliding trajectory towards the ground;
The force of the crash was totally profound.

The engine landed on top of a four-foot boulder.
It had broken loose from the motor mounts,
The car bounced right back up into the air;
The concussion was mammoth, tantamount,
Like two planets colliding, exploding,
The impact felt as if I was imploding!
As the car was landing on the passenger side,

My hands were frozen to the wheel, trying to steer;
This had turned into one major Hell of a ride!
The calamity was not yet over, I feared.

A huge pile of boulders out there,
Were rapidly converging towards me.
I collided and careened into the air,
The landing was even more misery.
It was a high-flying, full-impact wreck!
The car finally crash-landed on the roof,
As the roof was crushed down
Firmly against the back of my neck,
I was just barely able to move;
I was very tightly jam-packed!

All of the glass windows were blown out.
I seemed to be feeling rather okay.
The dust was clearing from all about,
Quickly it had turned into a lousy day!

Sitting in my seat upside down,
I released my shoulder strap.
Rolling down onto the car's ceiling
Onto the broken pieces of glass,
My brain was opting for me what to do.
That's when I newly discovered
I had a cut on my forehead
And a deep laceration on my elbow,
It was very difficult, extracting myself
Out of the crunched-up, resized window,
I looked like a Hermit Crab from Hell,

Bloody and slowly crawling out of its shell.

A little ways out into the desert,
I took the beer and the empty cans,
And hid them behind a Saguaro cactus;
It really was not much of a plan.
I knew it wouldn't take an Indian
Very long to follow my tracks;
A short ways from the accident,
People were stopping and starting to chat.

But at least for me, the evidence
Might not possibly go to a trial.
Because it came from a bit of a distance,
I could conceivably have a plausible denial.
A few had witnessed the crashing rollover;
Hanging around, still half expecting a show.

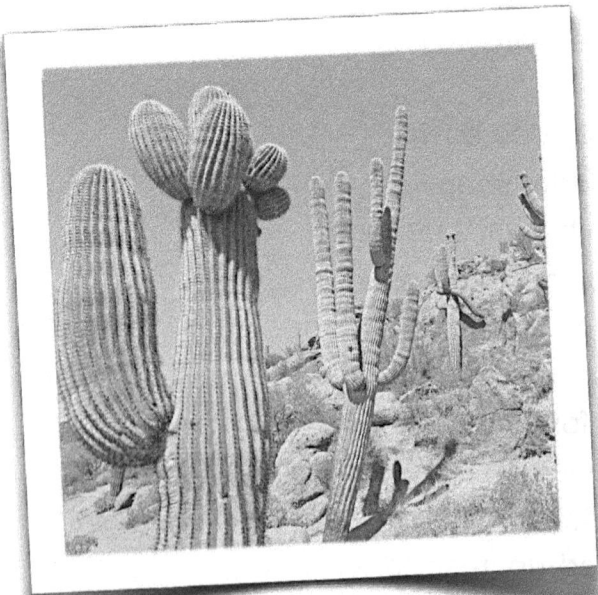

Someone had called the Sheriff with their CB radio.
No one would agree to giving me a lift,
I would have ditched my car, lickety-split,
Instead I was foggy, trying to gather my wits.

The Sheriff asked if I thought I would be wanting
To go to the Mexican Hospital down the road.
My occipital lobes really felt like exploding,
But I emphatically stated, "No Señor, no!"

My elbow was bleeding,
It had a short-but-deep laceration.
I had sustained two cracked and broken ribs.
I said I was fine, because I had reservations -
My friends had previously warned me -
To stay out of their hospitals,
If you really wanted to live.

Their clinics were infamous
For using infectious needles;
I did not want to catch Hepatitis,
Or Staph or Syphilis or Measles.

He said, if my automobile
Wasn't Mexican-insured,
I was going directly to jail,
To be a Mexican Jailbird.

I said,"Here is my paperwork,
I am fully covered,
At the border, I bought Seguros Tepeyac,

The best one, out of all of the others."

He said,"I am giving you a ticket
It will cost you right now, 40 dollars."
I agreed; I felt I had been complicit.
He looked angry and hot under the collar.

"Okay,"I had managed.
He motioned, with his fingertips rubbing,
(All this was spoken in
Broken English and Spanish)
"What are you waiting for?" he said,
"Right now, give me the money!"

I showed him that I was waiting
For him to write me the ticket,
Naively anticipating that he was legit.
He said,"Do you want to go to jail?"
I opened my wallet and I gave him the cash;
He wasn't going to leave a paper trail.
He said,"Get in the car, and I'll take you on back."

2 DETAINED

We got in his beat-up, old '52 Ford,
Went down the highway for a while.
Then he turned off onto a dirt road
Sagaciously concealing his evil guile.
Nervously I looked all about,
There was absolutely nothing there.
Then he told me to get out,
He was the Law; I had nothing to fear.

He opened his door and deliberately got out.
As he slowly walked around the side of the car
From his holster he pulled out his revolver.
It was starting to get seriously dramatic;
There was a sense I wouldn't be going too far.

He pointed his gun as he walked up behind me,
Waved his trusty pistol right at me,
Indicating for me to get down on my knees.
Stood back far enough - too far, unable to reach -
I was starting to panic, I just couldn't believe!
He put his gun to the back of my head.
I was so stunned at all of the absurdity -
How swiftly one could end up dead
From a minor traffic emergency!

I was completely astonished -
There was no time to even cry -
He talked really fast in Spanish;
I was shocked, that I was going to die!

I truly did not have a clue.
Why I was a dead man, I really could not tell.
There was nothing that I likely could really do,
But I cursed this vile man to Deep, Darkest Hell!
He ranted at me, then he tried acting cool.
He finished his pathetic, sermon-like spiel.
This Mexican Prick was incredibly cruel.
But he still was not done with his deal.
He told me to get back up,
Get back into the car.
Wide-eyed, I looked up,
This Pig was bluffing so far.

I was mute, I didn't say a word.
He drove me to this rustic hacienda,
Even further on out in the desert;
I was about to get the Rest Of His Agenda.

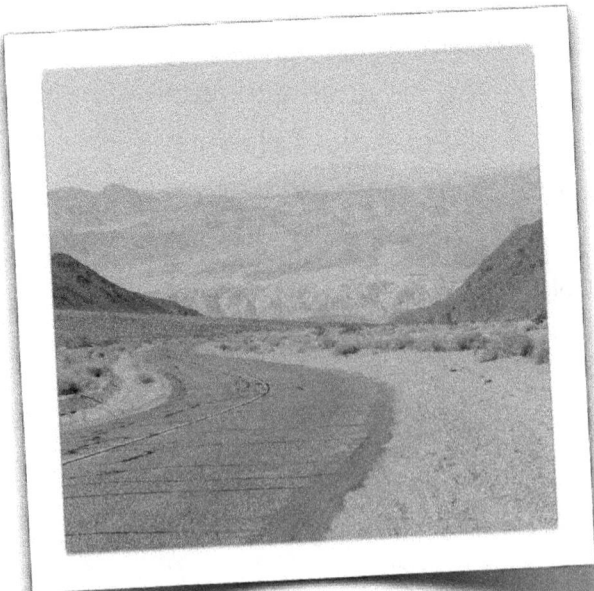

It had a counter and stools,
And this really-decrepit old lady
At a stone hearth, was cooking food,
With very hot sauces and gravy.
The Cop asked if I would like some water,
Then he nodded to the old woman,
And she haggardly waddled on over,
Brought me a capped bottle,
It was Gringo-safe water
It was sealed and carbonated;
In Mexico you only drink bottled water,
Their tap water is always contaminated.
She made me a chicken burrito.
I said,"Gracias," my hunger was sated;
But about this malevolent Cop,
I was not glad, gratified or placated.

Appearing amiable for over an hour,
I sat listening to his diatribe, unending.
His display of Civil Service Power,
Was overdone, pompous, and pretending.
I kept my mouth shut, eyes not looking up,
Not asking any contentious questions.
I did not, at all, want to piss off this Cop,
Smiling, I indulged all of his dispensations.
He told me to get back in the car,
"I'm taking you back to Sonoyta,
That's where I'm dropping you off.
From there you can catch,
The bus back to Mexicali;
It won't take you long to get back."

3 RELEASED

Recently almost memorialized,
I was still in a state of shock,
As I most thankfully entered
The roadside restaurant-bus stop!
To get back home to Santa Rosa,
I had to carefully watch my money.
But I was bursting with joy, Feliz Dias!
Suddenly Life was Bright and Sunny.

I saw this white woman at a booth all alone,
Traveling with peasant-poor Mexicans.
I asked her what it was that she had going on,
She said she was working on her Doctorate.
She matriculated from Berkeley's Cal. University,
She was doing some kind of
Anthropological study
On Mexican economic adversity.

She had heard from her friends,
While we were waiting for the bus,
That the cops were tearing my car to shreds;
The gossip was creating quite a fuss.
Apparently the Policía were thinking that
I was some kind of Big-Time Drug Smuggler!

We made friends, and talked quite a lot,
But not soon enough, could I wait to leave there.
She refused to sit next to me,
When we got onto the bucket-of-bolts bus;

I sat two-thirds of the way down the aisle,
Towards the back of this old oil burner;
I was glad I was leaving Sonoyta behind!

We went about 20 miles, then I had more bad luck.
Soldiers were in the back of a buckboard farming truck,
Forming a roadblock using bright yellow flashing lights;
It was most likely not going to be my best night.

Full of guys looking pretty tough,
Wrapped with bandoliers and carrying rifles,
They were obviously mean and rough.
Wearing white pajamas and sandals,
And old, faded straw hats, funny stuff!

One soldier got onto the bus by the driver.
He pointed his rifle straight towards the back,
Announced that coming aboard was an officer.
Then this little skinny guy, in his crisp, Nazi-like uniform,
He walks right on past by,
Nose high with militaristic scorn.

He headed towards the back of the bus;
I had a moment of pause from my grief;
Thank God he was after someone else!
I exhaled a Big Sigh Of Relief.
Then he returned to the front of my seat,
Reached to the luggage rack up above,
Then he swiftly opened my suitcase,
Stuck his hands in, all over the place,
Giving my clothes the once-over.

"Hey that's mine!" I stood up.
He swiftly had quick-drawn his pistol,
Banging the barrel into my forehead,
Lickety-split, it looked like an old German Luger,
Again, the absurdity
Of possible, nonsensical, sudden death!

He said something nasty to me in Española,
I put my hands up and slowly sat down,
While he was still holding that Luger to my head,
But there was nothing in my bags to be found.

He turned around and they exited;
And that is all that there was,
Until we got back to Mexicali,
I seemed to finally be done with the Fuzz.

What did not make any sense at all -
What I personally wanted to know -
Is why these morons would think
That I would smuggle drugs into Mexico?

Walking around in the dark in Mexicali,
I ran into these two red-headed white guys.
I was thinking that they were from the U.S.
"Can you please help me find
A cheap place to rest my eyes?"
It turned out they spoke very good English,
But they were indigenous from Mexico City.
I asked them to show me a hotel that was cheap;
I needed some sleep, I was starting to feel giddy.

318

They took me to this little, glass-fronted lobby;
I got a key to a room for only four dollars.
With one set of stairs going up to the next floor,
I was starting to hear voices of female callers.

As I got to the top of the stairs,
There must have been about twenty
Very attractive young girls;
I was a little afraid,
And I didn't have any extra money.

A long hallway going left, full of doors,
And also the same thing, going off to the right,
This is where I was going to spend the night,
Next to a room full of Mexican Whores.
It was very easy to distinguish
That half of those girls were white;

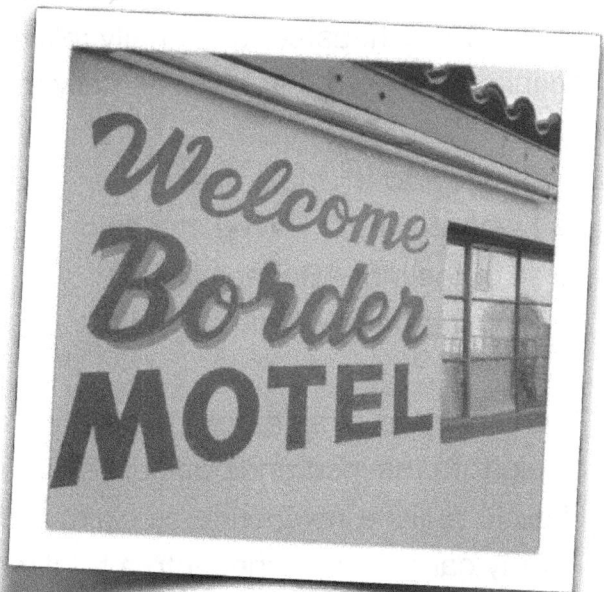

But they didn't speak any English,
Seemed odd, atypical, not-quite-right.
I assumed from where they had come,
Probably kidnapped early as children,
Never again seen north of the border,
From where they had originally,
Long ago been kidnapped or stolen.

Laughing and smiling,
I tried to get past,
While they were playfully grabbing
My crotch and my ass.
I scooted down the hallway,
Locked the door to my room;
I wanted some sleep before day,
Have a shower and get groomed.
Then I rolled out my sleeping bag,
On the dried-splooge-covered blanket,
Laid down exhausted, and finally relaxed,
Thanked the Lord that I had actually made it.

Slept late into the next day.
As I was leaving, I waved and said
To all of the girls "Buenos Dias,
I'm coming back when I get paid!"

Then I headed straight for the border,
Straight to the insurance office, Teyepac.
I had to register my insurance claim order,
For my car getting turned into a total wreck.

My totaled limit was 2000 dollars;
I wanted that compensation reimbursed.
I had paid for that much coverage,
I wanted my settlement to be disbursed.

The Agent sang to me that Corporate Song.
He told me I could go on home,
That it would not take very long,
Before I got a check in the mail,
From the Headquarters in Mexico City;
He was sure it would come without fail.

Entreating and exhorting me,
Somehow I managed to believe.
Crossed the border at Mexicali,
Sadly, I was still young and naive.
Returning to Santa Rosa, California,
I rode back on the Greyhound Bus,
Eating very little, most sparingly,
Because I only had a few extra bucks.
I finally got home, famished, but wiser.
I slept for two days, in between eating food,
Until it was time to return back to school.
I was trying to finish my second semester;
The check never came and my anger just festered!

I was angrily processing
His double-talk on the phone,
I was getting extremely inflamed,
At having to play his stupid game,
And now it was time to make him Atone!

4 RECOMPENSE

No more clowning around;
Exasperated, I loaded up my new used van,
And decided to go back on down.
Confront that Mexican Crook once again.

Get in his face, be obnoxious, and refuse to go.
Tell Tepeyac that I am demanding my money.
I kept my wheels on the U.S. side in Calexico,
I was just a pedestrian walking over to Mexicali.

The insurance office in that poverty-stricken town,
From the U.S. border was only two doors down.
It was very simple to just keep hanging around,
He thought I was a punk kid, just a young clown.
I demanded my money
From this insurance guy,
But he refused, glumly,
Hardly even tried to lie.

I had brought food from the U.S. just for a sit-in,
And I parked my ass in his leather recliner chair;
For his afternoon siesta, it was his favorite seat,
From there I could see anyone coming up the street.

I would warn naive, trusting Americans,
Who just came in to enquire there,
As I comfortably put up my feet.
I would deter them from buying insurance,
And tell them my dismal, sad, tragic story.

Earnestly warn them of rejection in advance
About the Company's defiant, noncompliant stance.

I was having fun, maliciously driving
All of his business away,
Revealing his slimy conniving;
The Company's refusal to pay.

First he tried calling the Cops on me.
As I was watching them come up the street,
I had plenty of time to jump to my feet.
Swiftly run back across the U.S. Border.
Those U.S. Border guys were so very cool;
They helped me by cooperating,
Because I had told them exactly
Ahead of time, what I was trying to do.
The Tepeyac Agent would then call the Federales;
Of course they were always too slow.

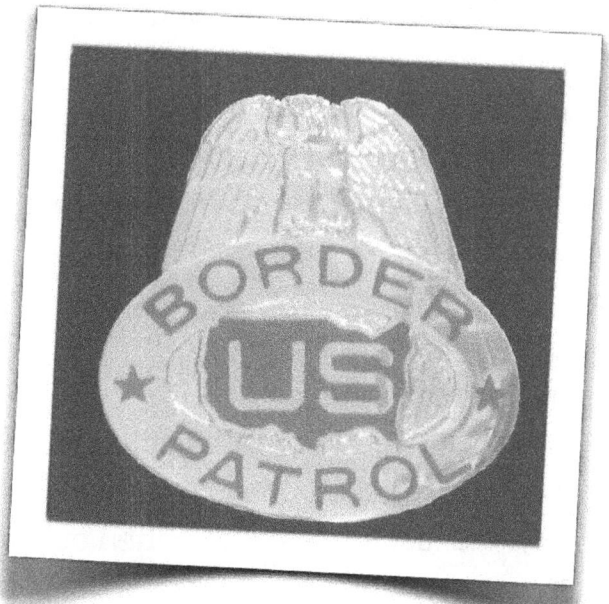

I jumped up, and dashed away quite easily;
Then returned to harass this Crook continuously.

His lazy, procrastinating indolence!
He felt he didn't have to recompense
Supposedly-rich American travelers;
It was his only excuse for being a Double-Dealer,
A defrauder, a scoundrel, a con artist and cheater.

I told him,"You are a Son of a Beeech!
There are just a couple of things,
For you that I am going to teach.
There are a few Yankees who sting,
And everybody is always within reach.

Before I am all through with you,
I might send you home to your wife,
Covered all over in black and blue,
To implore you to change your life.

You better cut me that check;
It is the only option you have left.
I've got the time to keep bugging you;
It would be the sensible thing for you to do."

He finally cut me the check.
I gave a curt thanks,
And I sauntered to the Mexican Bank;
The Cops wouldn't chase me anymore,
They had lost interest and gotten quite bored.

324

I did not trust the check not to bounce at a U.S. Bank,
And I wasn't leaving without my money.
He had no one but himself to thank.
Just as I was leaving, I popped in, calling him a Dummy.
He had customers, and I tauntingly waved the money;
He cursed me in Spanish to get out of his place.
I gave him the finger and said,"Fuck you!" to his face.

In the past 42 years,
I have not crossed the border,
Where the police are corrupt; no justice, just disorder.

I do not ever plan to go there again,
Back to that Hot-Peppered Pothole,
Way down south, it's still called Mexico,
Where life can be so fleeting, gone pronto!

WOLFGANG (A Teutonic Tale)

1 THE DREAM

Back in the spring
Of 1972,
I was hanging out with
My Brother-in-Law's Brother;
We were wondering what
We were going to do.
So we lit up a few,
While contemplating the upcoming summer;
And our favorite new saying was,
"Oh, what a Bummer!"

I was just now completing,
My first year of college,
Just brimming all over,
With lots of new knowledge.
Slick was tired of his low-paying,
Most-unrewarding, dead-end job.
We fantasized about tropical beaches,
Roasting pig and eating corn on the cob.

Originally how our brainstorm was formed,
I am not really quite sure,
But backpacking all summer in Hawaii
Was our solution; it was our Vacation Cure.

We did lots of planning,
A lot of Metsker-Map scanning.

326

With the young ladies from school,
We did a little pre-tanning.

Anticipating that it would not be very long,
Until we would be singing along,
Like Bob Hope and Bing Crosby,
Dignified, reclining under palm trees,
In freely-swinging fishnet hammocks,
Puffing on pipes and wearing
Red crushed-velvet smoking jackets.

Being fanned by palm fronds
Held by voluptuous Wahinis,
In erotic, little skimpy bikinis,
Romantically singing along,
To amorous "Ba-ba-ba-boo" songs.

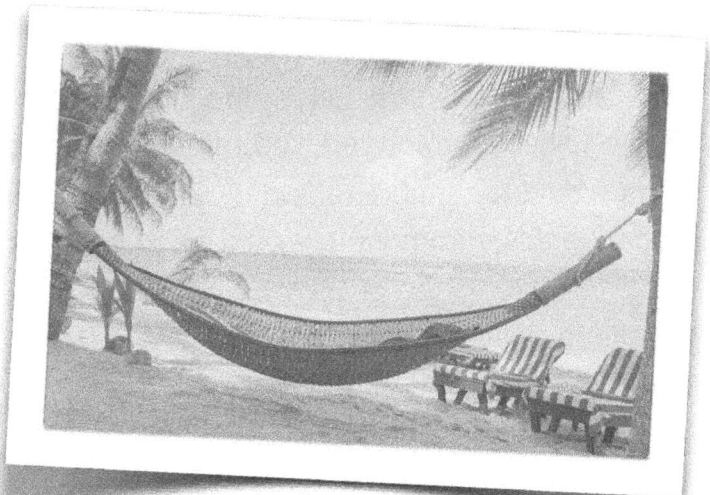

2 THE JOURNEY

Slick's brother and my sister
Were our auto transport
To the San Francisco Airport;
To Departures, we were promptly delivered.
We checked in our backpacks,
Which contained all of our food and our clothes.
Our lives were stuffed into those bags,
It made us quiver;
The thought of losing those packs,
It gave us a shiver.

Stuffed with swim fins, spearguns, snorkels,
And airtight face masks with a rubber nose,
For this temporary, off-the-grid escape;
Avoiding the Draft Board is what we chose.
We had not yet been selected,
And thought it might be a good idea,
Not to leave any forwarding addresses;
Just to take a long trip and disappear.

Now for more than ten years, the vile Vietnam War
Was endlessly prolonged, protractedly dragging on,
Feds would be unable to find us for induction,
Because this summer we would be absent, long gone.

Our flight delivered us to Waikiki.
We quickly transferred planes,
To the Big Island of Hawai'i,
Flying through torrential rains.

We had caught Hawai'ian Airlines
To the airport at Hilo;
It was the very last flight,
It was an Inter-Island Hopper;
When we arrived, they were closing the Airport.
And to us, the Airport Security Cop said,
"Leave here, move on, get out of my sight!"
On a very dark and inundatory, rain-filled night.

No streetlights, no traffic,
On a dark, two-lane road;
Depressing, to say the least,
As we dejectedly shouldered our load.
We had on Army rain ponchos,
We managed not to get soaked,
But it was at this moment of stress,
That my partner emotionally broke.
The desperation in his voice,
It gave me no choice.
He was weeping and could only speak
In a tremulous, trembling voice;
We couldn't go on, we had no choice.

His emotions were undoubtedly troubled.
We wandered off into the thick jungle vines,
Hastily set up an instantaneous camp;
Caught forty winks as we got through the night.
Our sleeping bags had become thoroughly damp,
And our gear was moderately soaked,
But we had a deliverance in the early morning;
Fortunately for us, the rain clouds broke.

We caught a ride
To the 480-foot high,
Very beautiful Akaka Falls.
They were preciously magnificent,
And so very incredibly tall.
It was just a picnic-style day park,
And no one else was anywhere to be found,
So we rolled out our sleeping bags,
To let them dry in the sun on the ground.

We spent the day eating,
And just hanging around,
And no Rangers appeared,
Before this fine day was done.
So we slept on the tables,
And not on the ground,
During dawn's early rising,
We just quietly moved on.

3 OUR FIRST GREAT ADVENTURE:
MANTA RAYS AND A SUMPTUOUS BUFFET

We shouldered our packs on our backsides,
Displayed our thumbs upward, to the sky,
Because we were heading to the Kona side,
It was time that we left the Windward side.

Into the desert on the Leeward side,
Through the great Palmer Ranch, we did ride.
It was the second largest cattle ranch of all,
In the entire US; vast, very substantial.
We stopped in at their butcher shop display,
And bought a couple of fat, juicy steaks.
Then on to the Kona Coast,
To search for a nice camping place.
In Hawai'i, it was nice to have no worries
About sleeping with poisonous snakes.
We went to heavenly Hapuna State Park,
And dejectedly found out
There was no camping allowed,
Not anywhere in the park;
Camping was Verboten After Dark!

We started to hike,
Northward, up the coast,
In the direction of
The Mauna Kea Beach Hotel,
Laurence S. Rockefeller's most-expensive resort
In his chain of Five-Star Hotels.
For the price tag of only $15 million,
It was the most extravagant resort in existence,

Back when it was built in 1965.
We showed up like The Beverly Hillbillies,
We made a grand entrance, The Boys Had Arrived,
To what was now the most-exorbitant hotel,
At that time, on the planet, for anyone to dwell.

We happened upon a rocky ravine,
It was a naturally-concealed grotto,
Where hardly anything could be seen;
Stealth And Secrecy was our status-quo motto.

We hid, hemmed in, just a ways back,
Amongst a pile of lava boulders;
We could not be spotted,
Nor exposed or discovered;
No direct line of sight from anywhere,
Except from the air;
Making it most imperative,
To disguise with our Surplus Army Ponchos.
Our rock shelter was secluded,
In our comfy, indistinguishable lair.
So we spread out our ponchos,
Across the top of the boulders.
It completely camouflaged us,
With our shiny white shoulders,
From any aircraft up above.

But best of all was the shade,
On those hot, sunny days.
What was there not to love?
Our outdoor bathroom facility,

Was a dirt hill with a shovel.
It was conveniently located
A respectable distance behind,
Our humble, little cozy hovel.

One of our early daily routines,
To where we would often depart,
Were the modern bathroom facilities,
That we could use during the daytime,
At the gorgeous, conveniently-located
Exotic, ocean-side Hapuna State Park.

In front of our new humble, earthy abode
Was an idyllic and scenic rocky cove,
Brimming full with schools of tropical fish,
A varietal seafood dining treasure trove!

With fresh and clean
Drinking-fountain water,
We filled our canteens,
Checked out the scene;
Cruised the girls on the beach.
But we remained mostly unseen,
Carefully staying clean out of sight,
Late afternoon, long before it fell dark;
Rangers standing on the ridge were scanning the beach,
With binoculars, they could view the whole park.

We did a little reconnoitre,
And soon happily discovered,
We were on the edge of the border;
Right between the hotel golf course
And Hapuna State Park.

At night we would walk,
On the greens in the dark,
Picking up ripe, coconuts.
We had a fresh sweet new ingredient,
To mix in our breakfast granola;
It was a tasty added nutrient.

We each had one set of dress clothes,
For spiffing up our appearance after dark.
Wide-eyed, around the hotel we would wander,
As if we were guests, chins up, we would saunter.
We would visit the statue of Buddha at night,
Steal the change from his cupped, open hands;
Coins placed with wishes from young lovers,

Cast forth, into the night-time desert sands.

Buddha whispered, "Look over my right shoulder,
At this luscious tree full of limes.
Take them back to your camp,
Sprinkle some on your barbecued fish,
So mouthwatering, they taste mighty fine."

One day we were snorkeling
Our way up the coast,
When a Giant Manta Ray
With a twelve-foot wingspan,
Swam ten feet below me;
Glided by like a submarine-winged boat!

It left me stunned and quite shaken,
I panicked and swam awestruck,

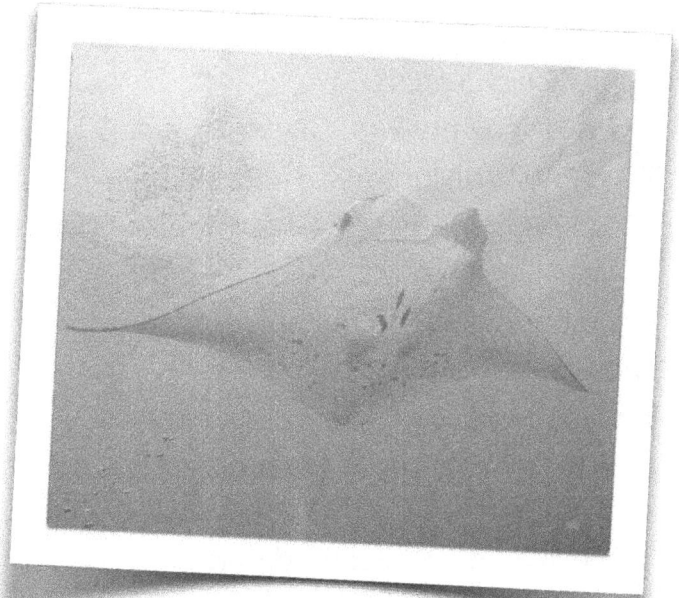

I was completely intimidated;
It was so massive and stout.
That giant creature left me agape;
It utterly freaked me out!

Later we perceived
There were many more Giant Rays,
Whirling and reeling,
But never careening.
Like swimming-pool vacuums,
Filtering out the sea plankton;
Straining through the ocean,
For microbiological life.

But in between gulping down
Minuscule, tiny sea particles,
Gliding effortlessly, they lapped up
The exceedingly-elegant,
So uncommonly-upscale,
Super-Chic cuisine,
It was all so very First Class;
The Hotel's delightfully delectable,
Scrumptiously, most-savory Kitchen Scraps!

It is most difficult to conceive,
The full size of these creatures,
Up close one is shocked and stunned,
So astounding, you just cannot imagine!

It was like an undulating parade,
From a Homecoming Pageant,

Of gigantic floats, just meandering by.
With underwater spotlights,
Mounted on the seawall,
Shining luminously at night.
It was all so very fascinating,
Visually engaging, most captivating!

Those immense Manta Ray sightings,
Like airplanes, circling and gliding,
A water performance with stage lights,
For the tourists' entertainment,
And their own viewing pleasure;
Long into the sparklingly, starry night.

One day, a boy of about sixteen,
Was hanging out by our cove;
We drifted out of the shadows, unseen.
We were wondering what he was doing;
We were somewhat curious to know.

His Father was a dentist from LA,
At the Hotel was where they did stay,
With his Mother and the five girls,
There wasn't much more he could take.
He said, "They are driving me crazy,
I just had to get away."
We said, "Okay."
We were thinking of exploring,
Going south, down the coast;
"Would you want to take a short journey,
A half of a day at the most?"

We traveled fast, up and down;
The kid had good feet on the ground.
We had a very good time;
Brought him back to our camp,
For some fresh fish, simply seasoned
With some of Buddha's donated limes.

He said, "For you guys,
If you come by our suite tomorrow,
I'll have a tasty breakfast surprise.
My father never checks the check,
He never takes the time to analyze,
He just casually endorses the bill.
And I am more than quite sure,
If you put on your good clothes,
And you bring some big appetites,
Then come knock on our door,
After all of my family vacates,
Has left and already gone down,
To the Hotel Dining Room,
Then you both will be able to gorge!"

"I will call Room Service,
No need to be nervous;
We will have a big breakfast,
With all of the fixings,
On the Lanai in our room,
Right after my family has left us,
And gone downstairs for breakfast."
Our timing was impeccably perfect.
Just as we began evacuating

Through the steel double doors,
The family was stepping out of their room,
And continuing onto the elevator,
With all of the young girls, each and every last one;
This breakfast buffet was really going to be fun!

Room service delivered,
Exactly on time,
Just like the kid had said,
It was satisfaction sublime!

We plowed right on through,
That lush, tropical banquet
Like a stampeding buffalo herd.
It turned out that this admirable kid,
Was every bit, as good as his word!

4 BAD TURTLE JUJU
AND FRUSTRATED PARK RANGERS

The next day I dove down,
And saw a giant green Sea Turtle,
It must, at least, have had,
A five foot-long shell.

With the point of my spear gun,
I lightly poked him
In the back of the head.
He panicked in a flurry,
He scrambled and scurried,
I looked into his bottomless eyes,
And saw his deep fear of dying.
As he frantically swam away from me,
I think I may have gathered up,
Some very bad juju you see;
It may have attached itself to me.

I may have damaged my Karma,
With Sea Turtle Spirits, irreparably!

The local natives then warned me:
"More sooner than later, Evil is coming for you;
It is entirely possible that bad omens,
Unleashed from the depths of the ocean,
Very soon will harass, and start following you!"

By the campfire one night,
I stood up to stretch in the dark.
I saw the Park Rangers coming,
For us, with flashlights, from the Park.
Quickly, we extinguished the fire;
As we watched in the dark,
At what rapidly transpired,
We readied quickly to embark.

Tragically for them,
The Park Rangers had lost
Their guiding beacon of light
On that black, misty night.
They started wandering in circles,
In the thick, heavy brush,
In Kiawe thorn bushes,
Sharp spiny cactus and such.

We were quite entertained,
We were laughing, restrained;
They were quite a comical sight,
Aimlessly meandering in circles,

Much to our merry delight!

We knew they were hot,
Perspiring and dirty,
They must have been
Scratched and bruised;
We knew they were hurting.

They were verbally graphic,
But we were not sympathetic.
Unforgiving, we thought that
It had just served them right,
For surreptitiously sneaking around,
In the bush trying to apprehend us,
On this spooky, dark, cloudy night.

They were incensed, irate and enraged,
Cursing and swearing, fuming, inflamed.
It was very exciting; Oh, what a doozy!
Like watching the Keystone Cops,
In a very old-time silent movie.

They got lost and confused,
There was almost a fight.
They could not get their bearings,
Without the incandescent emanations,
From our now-extinguished,
Efflorescent campfire light.

One day I was reading my Bible,
While lounging on the slippery rocks.

I was watching Slick with one eye,
While he was making a Dinner Dive.

Spearfishing in the cove,
There were always fish nearby swimming
By the rocks where we dove.
Suddenly, from under the water,
His hand reached out and grabbed onto a rock,
He yanked himself out of the water;
Like a seal, he was out like a shot!

A Tiger Shark had just made a charge;
It was extremely frightening and very large.
Undeniably, understandably,
Slick was agitated, and terror-stricken;
We were both extremely alarmed!

As time went on, we further began to worry.
Somehow it felt like we should leave in a hurry.
Like we had just worn out our welcome.
Now maybe it was time, and then some,
That we should be urgently moving along.
Promptitude before procrastination;
It was becoming much more apparent,
We needed a new, propitious destination.

In daytime the Rangers,
Maybe sooner than later,
Might remember their ire;
The disappearance of our campfire.

Choosing the daytime,
To come looking around,
We would prefer to avoid them;
It was becoming nerve-wracking,
Not to utter, or make any sounds.

We had now surmised,
That maybe it was time,
To return back to town,
With all of our gear,
Load up on pizza and beer,
And try to gain back a few pounds.

We decided we would use some discretion,
And appreciate not having been found.
Leaving behind no scraps or remnants,
We carefully policed all of the grounds,
Then we gave thanks and remembered the lesson.

So we packed up our things,
And regretfully we walked,
Out to road, with boots on the ground,
Out to the asphalt highway at dawn,
Hitchhiking our way back to town.

5 ARCHANGEL GABRIEL
AND HIS WEIRD HIPPIE CHURCH

We hitchhiked 160 miles,
With thumbs reaching out;
Our faces flashing big, happy smiles.
Hitchhiking to Hilo on the Windward side,
People were always so kind and friendly
In those days, generously giving us rides.

We had no idea of a domicile;
We knew of no other place we could go,
Trusting that opportunity would show;
What that would be, we did not know,
We did not have any plan,
We were totally beguiled.
Hitchhiking with our backpacks,
We had no bills, nor any rent,

No job, very few cares.
Chewing on sugarcane,
By the side of the road,
Ruminating just where,
We were going to find an abode.

Up walked this giant blond guy,
He announced himself,
And introduced us to Hawaii,
Like a deacon, or a game show host;
He was much stronger and larger than me,
And I am much taller and larger than most.

He said he was the Reincarnation
Of the mighty Archangel Gabriel;
He was a Holy Spirit, not a ghost,
From the wheat-growing fields of Palouse.
A farm boy, tired of cutting and baling hay;
A handsome behemoth, as big as a moose!
To Hawai'i he came to sermonize and orate,
He arrived here sometime last year,
Emigrated from Lewiston, Idaho;
That was quite a revelation to hear!

He started Preaching the Lord,
Killing our chances of getting a ride,
So we accepted his invitation to dinner,
And a place to sleep on the floor inside.
It was fun at first,
Being in this weird Hippie Church.
The leaders were these four,

Very strange, unusual guys;
They were running a home
For destitute single mothers,
Whose children were all under five.

As they woke us up for the Morning Bible Lessons,
We were flirting and winking with the girls on the sly.
There was this insane, really demented guy,
An obsessive and frustrated manipulator.
He had been outside in the yard, casting out the Devil,
From his now-nearly-defunct, rusty carburetor,
Because his truck just couldn't be told
How to send gas to the intake manifold!

Measuring with a standard carpenter's level,
We gauged him to be at least two bubbles off.
We were heading out for the evening,
Hopefully to debauch women, party and revel.
Eyeballing us, he had suspiciously detected,
That his supposed spiritual powers,
And all of his exhorting and admonishing,
By us, was not really believed or respected.

Heading out for some pizza and beer,
Smoking our stash of Pakalolo,
We stayed out pretty late,
Partying in fourth gear.

After a few days of that,
The girls delivered sad rumors.
We were to be swiftly expelled,

For having unforgivably rebelled;
We accepted it all in good humor.
Except for that part where they said
We were in cahoots with the Devil.
How swift and unforgiving they were,
To banish our sorry asses to Hell!

Back out in the streets,
We devised a new plan.
Lots of condemned, empty houses
That had been built up on stilts,
Many standing alone, clean and empty;
So many vacancies left to be filled.

Nice and clean on the inside,
Just waiting for vagabond vagrants
To have a place to abide and reside.
But when the volcanic quaking,
Had the houses wiggling and shaking,
We were alert, always ready—
If the house was unsteady—
To swiftly jump out of the windows,
Land on our feet, somersault and roll.

A neighbor woman saw our avocados
Ripening out on the roof.
She called the Police, we were arrested,
But their noses were mightily tested;
They didn't want to take us in.
They told us to go to the beach,
And take long showers instead.

We tried, but they'd lied—
There were no showers at the beach.
They refused to put us in their car,
Because we so badly reeked!
We wandered around,
Till we eventually found,
A public school, so we walked around back.
It was quite a fortuitous shock,
To find the doors left unlocked!
No one was to be seen anywhere around,
It was our little slice of Heaven,
We were so grateful to have found.

We headed straight for the locker room showers.
Clean and shaven, we walked into the sunshine,
Like a bouquet of freshly-cut flowers,
Fresh and scented and smelling so fine.

6 OUR SECOND GREAT ADVENTURE—KILAUEA

After lounging around for a few days,
We then embarked on our merry way.
Our new destination —
God's wondrous creation —
Was the big Kilauea,
Princess Pele's Volcano.

We were picked up by
A young, professional couple.
From New York City,
On us, they took pity.
We were safe for a ride,
We had been predetermined,
Unlikely to be any trouble.

Picked us on up, and then they confided,
Thought we were cool, they then had decided.
They previously had observed us,
When coming over on the plane;
They were both confidently sure,
That we were fairly safe and sane.

Inquisitively they asked us,
"What do you want to do with your lives?"
And we said, "This destination was our desire.
We have been trying to strive;
The enjoyment of living amongst Nature,
It makes us feel especially alive."

They asked us,
"Have you had any desire,
To come to New York?
You just cannot conceive!
It is so amazing,
It is oh, so grand!
You must come soon and see it,
The very first chance that you can."

We beamed and we blinked,
Then we looked all around us,
Grinning in total disbelief.
We no longer had any desire
To be completely surrounded
By massive mountains of concrete.

We had both made a break from Detroit,
Said goodbye to the filthy steel factories,
All the salt and the soot,
That was mixed in the snow,
That we so happily had escaped,
Over three years ago.
To move on to the West,
To escape out of the East,
By Golly, Good Grief!
It was such a welcome relief!

To go on to another
Over-polluted northern city,
To us, the idea was ridiculous;
It would have been such a pity.

New York was the last place,
That we never, ever wanted to go.
We said, "Please open your eyes,
Look all around you,
We are enveloped in Paradise!
And even sunny California,
Would not be such a bad prize.
But New York City, are you kidding?
To us it would be like Hell On Earth.
Really, get serious, c'mon guys!"

After they dropped us off
On the National Park Road
To the Kilauea volcano,
We hitched and hiked nonstop,
All of the way to the steamy top.

We stashed our packs in the brush,
Before we walked on over
And joined the rest of the bunch.
They were starting out on the trail,
Which wholly consisted
Of porous, bulldozer-crushed,
Crumbling, smashed lava rock.
So the unsuspecting tourists,
Would not break through the surface,
How deep they might fall far below!
The victim could plunge to depths unknown,
Descending into shadowy black holes
Made by flammable gas
Inside of the volcanic glass.

I wandered off of the compressed tractor trails;
Smoothly running across and all over,
On the obsidian hills and the Stygian dales.
Then I instantly broke through
One of those gas-pocket globules,
Exactly as I had been warned,
Ignoring, just having been told,
Of what I am supposed *not* to do.
Broken glass scraped off some of the skin,
The side of my ankle was hemorrhaging.

I was very lucky, my wound was only superficial,
But it bled all over the side of my sock.
It looked a lot worse than it was,
And it got me a stern, long lecture,
From the cute, Lady Ranger-Boss.
It is most impressive to tell,
Describing that Doorway To Hell.

One thousand feet down,
Fiery, flaming, swirling lava,
Orange quickly turning to black,
Occasional geysers, although far distant;
Still causing one to take a step back.

Leaving Nature's Amazing Display,
It was starting to get, very late in the day.
And although camping was not allowed,
We were in a giant National Park.
We drifted off of the highway,
Down a forest road, that was eerily dark;
And after a very wet mile,
Of walking through the rain forest park,
We came to an open clearing.

A totally abandoned, a sadly-neglected,
A fenced-in garden of dying orchids;
Relinquished, not taken.
There was a steel shed with locked doors,
That we easily removed off of their tracks,
Removed all of the fertilizers and pesticides,
Covered them in plastic, around in the back.

Built a small campfire,
Right in front of the door,
It was so incredibly comfortable,
We stayed there for two days more.
We were especially careful before we left,
To precisely put all of the garden things back.
We left no obvious traces,

We cleverly covered our trail,
So that only an experienced
Outdoorsman Tracker could tell.
No signs that anyone had lingered there;
That there had been two weary travelers,
Camping with heavy backpacks,
Enjoying the scenery, its ambiance,
And the pleasantly rich floral fragrance.

Reluctantly, returning from a tropical rain forest,
A leisurely stroll down the mountainside;
The beauty was absolutely astounding.
Walking amidst songbirds and butterflies,
Ingesting the scenery, we drifted casually on by;
Disinclined to be leaving that glorious high ground,
Craving pizza and beer, we headed right back to town.

7 HANGING OUT IN HILO TOWN

We hitched a ride back on a garbage truck,
Our hitchhiking choices, were the usual dumb luck.
The owner-driver, a large, hefty local guy,
Asked us if we would like to work for him;
Because he had no free time for his family,
None to play on the beach, none to swim.
The pay was most enticing,
But sadly we had to turn him down.
Although we appreciated the offer,
We left him with a disappointed frown.
We came here for a vacation,
Just for the rest and relaxation.
We weren't the type of guys to shirk,
But we had not come here to find work.

In September, I had to return back to college,
Slick would again have to find a new job,
So we wanted to maximize our vacation,
Up until the very last moment,
When we would have to leave with a sob.

Not yet time to leave Paradise behind,
Not yet ready to train and discipline my mind,
Not yet ready to apply myself to the Daily Grind,
Not yet ready to psyche myself up with concern,
Not yet time to focus, to study and learn,
We'll leave at the last minute that we discern,
For our mournful, melancholy, Mainland Return.

We returned to our Hilo gymnasium shower,
Then went on out to our Social Nirvana;
The coffeehouse style, beer and pizza parlor.
Renewed some acquaintances recently encountered;
So far the only place that we found at this date,
Where Haoles all performed, partied and ate.

Where we were able to find a safe harbor,
Where we were able to congregate.
Our own place to hang out,
If you had a white face.
An open mike for artistic expression,
We had laughter, boisterous derision.
A clamoring of humorous criticism,
A domicile for poets and musicians.
A refuge for Thespians to demonstrate,
Share their skills and their talents,
Tip a few beers, give a few cheers.
Sometimes it was difficult
To control and to manage;
Not to get carried away,
Not to overindulge,
Not to over-inebriate.

But soon It was time to find a new home,
A place that would not take us very far;
Somewhere close from where we could roam,
And still within walking distance to a bar.
So we walked a few blocks,
Searching towards the outskirts of town,
Looking for a nice, clean, condemned structure,

357

That the city couldn't afford to knock down.
For meals we would buy bread,
Miracle Whip and tomatoes.
From the neighborhood lawns,
The Locals had told us,
That it was more than okay,
To pick up any fallen, ripe avocados.

Such delicious sandwiches, we devoured!
In the morning for breakfast, and for lunch;
Sometimes we added cheese and cold cuts,
Which made them quite heavenly scrumptious.

After lunch we would head on over
To the old Woolworth 5 &10 Store.
Fantastic, phantasmagorical good news!
The lunch counter had premium Kona Coffee,
With unlimited refills.
And in some pretty counter girls,
We were absolutely thrilled!

When we walked out of that place,
We were filled to the gills.
The flavor was superlative,
Most impossible to resist.
We could not stop the swilling,
Always fulfilling, such java so rich!
The aroma, an exquisite emanation,
We could not desist, it was delectable;
We were absolutely elated.
The caffeine was stimulating,

Bursting outward and secreting,
From each and every single pore;
We just couldn't ask for anything more!

Then we would light up a spliff,
And walk on down to the shore.
Once again, often returning,
To the public school's back door.
We would hit the gymnasium bathroom,
And we took full advantage,
Of the hot, steaming showers once more.
Then we enjoyed hanging out
At the pizza parlor store,
Flirting with the Wahinis,
Making genteel efforts to score.

Life was becoming a little too perfect,
Everything was just gaiety galore.
We were losing our cutting edge,
We were starting to get fat and lazy;
The Pakalolo was keeping us spacey.
We had a jamming, jungle agenda,
We wanted to get back to our plans.
We were starting to lose sight, getting lazy;
Our focus was beginning to get hazy.
Neglecting the dream we were chasing,
We wanted to go back out in the wild again!
That was the intent of our original plan;
Post haste, we would depart in short order,
As promptly as time would allow or demand.

8 OUR THIRD GREAT ADVENTURE: WAIPI'O VALLEY AND BAPTIST JOHN

We hit the highway again,
With our thumbs pointing north,
Heading onwards towards Paradise,
As we merrily marched forth.

This time we were totally
Separating from Civilization.
There along the northern coast,
Was this idyllic town,
Honoka'a, a Utopian Destination.
Back in the day,
If you were in search of
The rare Macadamia Nut,
This was the place where you came,
This is how the town got its fame.

We followed State Highway 240,
Until the very end of the byway;
It was named Waipi'o Valley.
It was so incredibly quaint,
A beautiful picture to paint,
Astonishingly so full of charm;
And it had the last telephone
With which to sound an alarm.

We headed on out to the end of the road,
That was where the trailhead had its start;
It was the only place from where to begin,
For the backpackers to embark and depart.

An agglomeration of pleasant smells,
And an accumulation of visual charms,
Past a small village of taro root farms.

But it was already late in the afternoon,
We were going to run out of daylight,
So we had to march out very soon.

It was an incredibly steep climb,
Ten miles up over the top of the ridge;
Through thick, forested jungle,
Along the edge of the cliffs.
We followed the narrow donkey trail
Till we met a well-tanned young man;
We decided to stop and share travel tales.

He only wore only a pair of shorts,
And carried a rather thick,

Sturdy, big walking stick.
He had a patched and scruffy beard,
And a pile of brown hair.
What a thick, curly crop,
That he had crowning on top.

He told us that his name was John,
And he had been over in Vietnam.
We offered to share some of our food,
But this sensitive man from Virginia
Was serenely asserting with a friendly smile,
That the only food that he did eat
Was the fresh produce from the jungle;
All of the various fruits that grew in the wild.

So we bid him Adieu,
Daylight was burning,
It was time to proceed and move on.
We now had to start trekking,
No time to delay for a man without boots,
For a strange man that hikes while barefoot.

I couldn't help but compare him
To Jesus' cousin, the Baptist named John,
On the banks of the Jordan river,
Baptizing and preaching upon.

It got dark very fast,
In the jungle at night,
We were basically blind,
We had no eyesight.
362

It was becoming impossible
To pick up the trail.
I was afraid of a misstep,
And I said, "This is it;
I cannot see in the dark."
We were blocking the path,
Where we decided to park.

We spread out our sleeping bags,
On top of the trail, space was tight;
We zipped up, and said "Good Night."
We awoke early the next day,
The rising sun was adorning,
A raiment in rich golden rays,
Warming our bodies this morning.

But we had missed all of the warnings.
Still in our sleeping bags, we began to sit up.
We looked sideways, and just two feet over,
Holy Moses! Empty space! That was it!
The side of our narrow donkey trail
Abruptly dropped straight off of the cliff!

A couple of more steps,
From the edge of the ledge,
And our loving relatives,
Would have been mourning,
A couple of freewheeling,
High-flying, adventurous stiffs!

We packed up our gear,
As we ate some breakfast.
Then we quickly departed;
We thought we must be,
The first ones on the trail to have started.

Running and jumping,
Down the trail we charged,
Plowing through the brush,
We veered and we darted,
Sometimes almost jogging;
Directly into John's meditation location,
We had abruptly and recklessly barged.
We could not believe,
Our big, bulging,
Goo-goo googly eyes!
To see him there poised,
Into the lotus position,
It took us by total surprise.

Impossible it seemed,
That he could deftly maneuver,
In the darkness of night.
He had delicately tip-toed,
Then stepped right over our bodies,
We did not stir, we did not rise.
He could move like a ghost,
In the deepest dark blackness,
No flashlight, and still so close.
I don't know about you,
But what a shudder it gave us,
364

Just a wee bit of a fright.
How he could hike with no light?

We told Baptist John
That we were moving on,
And wherever we decide
To build our camp upon,
"You will always be welcome,
Wherever the trail turns,
Whenever our campfire burns."

With thanks he returned
To his focused meditation,
And we hurriedly descended
Into this magnificently resplendent,
Most grand, gorgeous valley,
Of fruit trees and flowers and ferns.

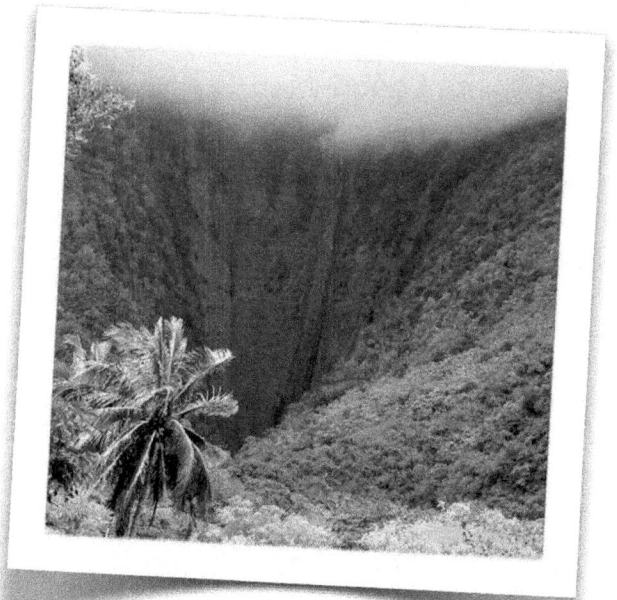

9 NAKED WOMEN!
THE CHURCH OF THE NUDE JESUS FREAKS

At the bottom of the valley
Was a substantially-sized, very-deep river;
Over our heads, too deep to ford,
A very swift current to cross.
But we were good swimmers,
And what we saw on the other side,
Well, we could hardly believe our eyes!

We could see about five naked women,
Their wet bodies shimmering and glimmering;
Also, to our dumbfounded surprise,
Just hanging around butt naked,
Were fifteen other guys.

We immediately dropped
Our jaws and our backpacks,
And swam across the rushing river.
In a spirit of good will
Our friendship was offered.
While they were having their dinner,
Three avocados on their dinner blanket, we spied.
"Please tell us, where is the tree that's not bare,
We will pick, and will generously share."

But with fear in their eyes,
They denied and they lied.
Then a special Japanese gal
Told us about a breadfruit tree,
A most excellent food.

If cut up and French fried,
Sprinkled with pepper and salt,
It could be really good!

What they didn't know,
As we borrowed their blanket,
And went off and got started,
Off into the woods we departed,
Was that my compadre, Slick,
Was a Tree Climber Extraordinaire;
And I could catch fruit like a baseball,
Snag it delicately out of the air.
Breadfruit, guava, mountain apples,
Avocados, papaya, and Mangos;
Swiftly we had already collected
A Fruit Blanket Supermarket!

With our many new fruit contributions,
We added a plethora of amiable friends.
But we still decided to live
On the other side of the river;
It was a better position to defend.

We moved into a half-walled
Abandoned Peace Corps Hut;
It was expeditiously convenient,
And charmingly comfortable enough.

It favorably suited our needs,
But we still had to kill
A few menacingly poisonous,

Brightly-colored centipedes.

Stepping right out onto the beach,
Lots of game fish within easy reach.
Palm fronds made our roof waterproof.
A mosquito-free, fresh-blowing breeze,
Passed over the half walls and under the roof.
Nature's Air Conditioning,
Blown in fresh from the sea.
We secured a safe homestead,
In which to reside;
Except for tsunamis,
A safe place to abide.
Our slightly decrepit, but newly-attained residence,
Had all that we needed, except for a white picket fence.

Right there on the beach,
We stacked flat lava rocks,

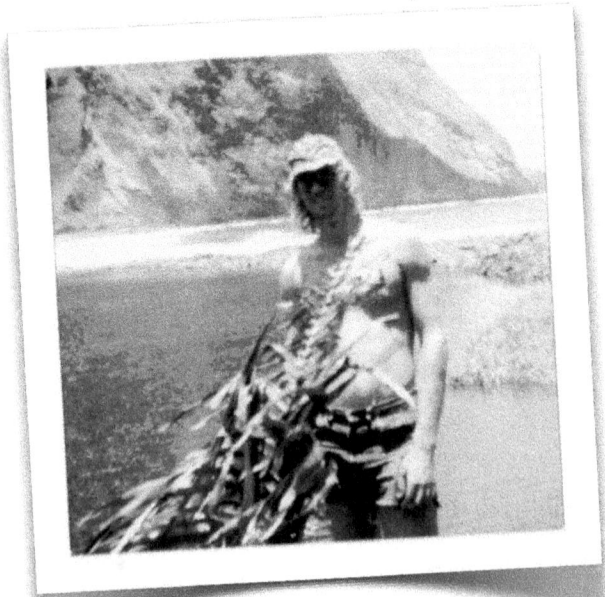

In an arching-over dome,
Going right over the top
Of our hot driftwood campfire.
We added a smaller dome up above;
A likeness of a pizza bread oven,
Built for the carbohydrates we loved!

And it wasn't too long before
We were eating warm bread.
And it tasted like Heaven;
Warm bread beautifully leavened!
Our beachfront Tiki-Hut domicile
Was dry, cozy and warm,
Out in the blustery, tropical wilds.

After a couple of days of meditating devoutly,
Baptist John came on down from the mountain;
He graciously stopped by for a visit.
Not discounting my imagination,
He seemed to be radiating a bit of a glow,
Barely detectable, emanating an aura,
The dude appeared to be sporting a halo!

Then we convinced him to try
Some of our whole wheat granola,
A combination of fresh fruit
And a little coconut slightly-risen bread.
Curiously we began hearing,
Some most distressing sounds.
Suddenly John had fallen to the ground,
Writhing in pain, squirming around.

369

Responding to our newly-homemade bread,
It had slammed into his stomach;
It felt like an ingot of hot, heavy lead.

After suffering for two hours,
He began to slowly recover.
He was going to be moving on,
North to the Honopue Valley,
Because in these parts around here,
There were just too many people to bear.
Sadly, I noticed his halo was gone;
Unfortunately it hadn't taken us long,
To accidentally do him wrong.

We profusely apologized,
For causing him such discomfort.
He said he had to expeditiously move on,
Because there was a very low tide.
Instead of climbing another mountain,
With much less of a trail than the other,
He would swim up the beach to the north,
Catching the surf rising out of the sea,
Around the point on to the next valley;
He would ride on the waves most easily.

I arose unusually early one morning
With that glittering, golden globe glowing,
Waves hitting my feet, my mind was wandering,
In the sandy, salty foam, I was beachcombing.
Barefoot this morning, the water felt cold,
The wet sand was squishing,

In between all of my toes.

Coming through the breakwater were four fishermen,
On a fishing boat, 24-foot-long outrigger;
Always a dangerous maneuver to try running,
It interrupted my concentrated treasure hunting.

They called for me to pull them through the surf,
To help them make a safe landing on the turf.
Standing in breakers, they threw me a rope,
Now you can just call me the Human Tugboat!

Four Asian-looking Hawai'ian guys,
Out trolling for fish in their boat's wake,
When soon they began to be followed,
By a large, seventeen-foot shark
Who was stealing all of their bait.

He was so monstrously huge,
And had aggressively bumped
Into the side of their wooden boat.
So they decided to beach,
Just for a couple of hours;
Not wanting to tempt Fate,
They took time out for a break.

For a while we watched the waves toil,
As we ate fish and rice wrapped in foil;
We kept watching the surf boil and roil.
I then pushed them in their boat back on out,
Against the lashing and crashing waterspouts.

Their boat was surrounded in white, creamy foam,
As they were heading on back to their families at home.

A few days later,
Three white guys from Ohio
Came down the mountain pass.
They stopped by our hut,
Very friendly and gave greetings,
But they left in a flurry, fairly fast.
The meeting was too fleeting to shake hands,
They were in such a hurry to join friends;
Right across the river, dancing cheek-to-cheek,
At The Church of The Nude Jesus Freaks.

So later on,
We brought fish and fresh bread,
To their celebratory party blast.
After dinner, across the river,
We dejectedly returned back.
But we were still thinking about,
Those good-looking five ladies,
And their cute, feminine derrieres,
At the same time blocking out,
Visions of nude men walking about.

10 OUT OF THE DARK, THE SHARK!

We arose early the next morning,
To a wonderful, wafting smell,
We swam back over the river,
They were cooking a pig; do tell!
The boys from Ohio
Had brought a .357 Magnum
In separate pieces on the plane.
They had hunted a pig early that morning,
Far back in the woods, trapped in his lair;
But they told us there wasn't enough,
And that they were not willing to share.

Chagrined by Human Nature,
Disappointed by the norm,
We decided to challenge
Mother Nature's windy storm.
It was time to go spearfishing,
But billowy black clouds
Were beginning to form.

Occasionally the vascular brilliance
Lightened the heavens with incandescence.
The explosive bursting and flashing,
The descending radiant ignition,
Illuminating veinlike white lightning,
As large waves were breaking,
At over eight feet tall.
Emotionally and physically,
It looked very breathtaking.

But 20 to 40 feet underwater,
Everything was quiet and serene;
Nothing unusual to be seen.
I had three fish already in my bag,
The hunting was good;
And it was beginning to look like
We would now have plenty of food.

Suddenly, I got punched
From behind my right shoulder!
That is the moment
When I laughed inside of my snorkel.
Slick was horsing around;
Aggression was our Detroit City Culture.
I swung my right elbow behind,
It locked and connected
With the corner of his mouth,
And he forcibly pushed me,
Like a boat, through the water!

He disengaged and turned on his side.
Quickly he rolled over,
He swam inches right beside,
With his mouth completely wide open,
Jagged jaws distended, extended!
Did a 90-degree turn,
Bouncing off of my chest,
Disappearing eerily into the emptiness.

It wasn't my buddy Slick,
But a ten-to-twelve-foot-long White Shark!
Oh man, he was fast!
With a wide-open mouth full of razor-sharp teeth,
Not a creature that you would ever want to meet!
He abruptly flew right on past;
I was overwhelmed and aghast!
Shocked, I was just barely coping;
Him not returning, I was just hoping.
My mind could not accept that I was just bait,
What I was seeing right in front of my face,
What I had observed,
Had not really registered.
What frightfully I had just witnessed,
Was a Killing Machine that teaches
Respect to the whole human race!

I could easily have shoved a basketball
Past double rows of teeth inside of his mouth.
He did an about 90-degree turn,
His body struck a glancing blow off of my chest,
Then he disappeared into the dark cloudiness,

Down the coast, as he was now heading due south;
Left me full of terror that he might return!
This Grim Reaper Of The Pacific Surf,
Unnerved, running into me on His Turf.

Thank God, he so swiftly headed away,
But I feared he might be circling about;
In my mind, all time was as if frozen.
And the dread of watching my speargun sway,
To the sandy rock bottom, as it went down,
While an inky black cloud was forming
Around my right arm and my chest,
Finally realizing that it was my own blood;
My essence, to the nose of this ravenous Shark,
The fragrance would be most delectable.
But now I was extremely detectable!

I turned over my arm,

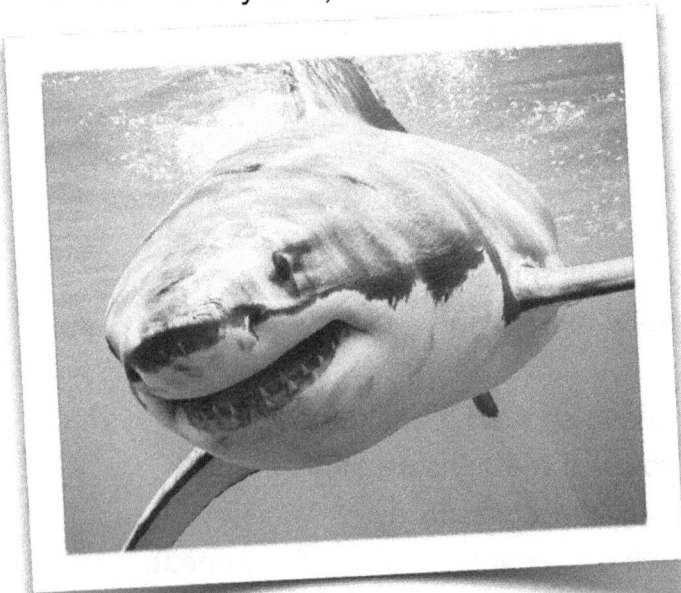

Two, four-inch-long gashes;
Blue muscle tissue was bulging out!
An eight-inch piece of skin, consumed
From my wrist, was now missing,
All of my arteries were exposed,
Quite a large amount was disposed!
I looked all around under the surface,
The water had become inky and cloudy,
I was surrounded by the impenetrable darkness,
Agitated, I hoped that the Shark had departed.

I raised my head above water,
In eight-foot-high breaking waves,
I frantically looked for Slick all about.
He was nowhere within sight,
I could not see beyond the next wave;
Time to concentrate on saving My Life!
I was deep and direly frightened,
As I was looking at my own exposed bone,
I felt so desperately all alone.

Being a young intellectual,
In these new modern times
I had often forsaken my God
Because of unjust war crimes.
Now at the first sign of danger,
And a little personal strife,
I begged God like a baby,
To save me, to protect me, My Life.
This terrifying epiphany
May possibly have rescued me,

From my previous spiritual destiny.

The experience that was mostly
Quite baffling to me,
Was the fact that my wounds
Were completely pain free.
But I could see that the saltwater
Was quickly draining my blood;
Drawing it out from my wounds,
A horrifying, torrential flood.
I rolled over onto my back,
Held my arm out of the water,
I barely could see,
Looking back over my head,
It was awkward not to gulp water.

The riptide, relentlessly,
Kept pushing me back out to sea;
I swam north at an angle,
To set myself free.
Agitated that my legs were exposed,
Worried he could bite them off, if I froze!
Fearing that the Beast would come back,
Bite and lacerate, cut, slash and hack,
Masticate my body, starting at my nose,
Right down to my toes, if he so decidedly chose.

The surf purged me out amongst the rocks,
Missing a swim fin, oddly I did still actually care.
I was a quarter mile north up the beach,
And I had very serious news to share;

I had to notify Slick of his endangerment.
Up and out of the water, it was a footrace.
I ran at full speed down the beach,
To the Jesus Freak Retreat.
I was drenched crimson in blood,
From the top of my head to my toes.
I found everyone lazily lounging there,
Still not wearing any clothes,
Their eyes opened wide as they stared.

I ran up to the campfire and screamed "Shark!"
Everyone panicked, they jumped up and scattered!
I said "Please come listen, come back quickly,
Please hurry immediately, we should!
We must get Slick out of the water,
Before he ends up as Shark Food!"

Then everyone ran down to the shore,
When they got in knee deep, they then froze;
Afraid to go any further, no deeper they chose.
So they jumped up and down,
Waved their arms all around,
Yelled as much as they possibly could.
Slick was playing out in the waves like a fool;
He seemed to have forgotten
The Buddy System Diving Rules.
He saw their commotion, people doing stunts;
All of the movement on the waterfront.
Oblivious that he had any danger in store,
He most casually swam on into the shore.
This lovely, naked Japanese girl,

(Another Guardian Angel, for sure)
Swiftly ran off to her tent,
She returned with a bag full of bandages,
And instantly, right to work she went.
She tied on a tourniquet,
Then she bandaged my bleeding arm;
To me, this girl was Heaven sent!
Her skin as smooth as white porcelain,
Like you would find on an antique button;
I was having fantasies about being the shirt
That she would be hand-sewn upon.
She most likely saved my very life,
No longer was I bleeding to death.
No more cause for serious alarm;
I was totally and childishly charmed.

The boys from Ohio
Speedily pulled on their boots,
Left their backpacks behind;
They promptly did scoot.
Back to Waipi'o Valley,
Over the mountain in only four hours;
An Amazing Accomplishment
That they completed on foot.
They promptly called the Police,
Who sent in a helicopter,
Which thankfully arrived, within the hour.
From above, two Japanese divers
Jumped into the water before the chopper landed,
Thinking that there might be dead bodies,
Floating in the waves, lapping.
380

Meanwhile, in shock I was telling my Life Story,
Just as if I was going to die before morning.

The helicopter returned us
To the Honoka'a Hospital;
Bouncing, swinging and swaying,
Just like a pail on a rope, we were flying.
To my surprise, the pilot was a very well-dressed
Gentleman Eskimo that was doing the driving.
Hastily I climbed up on the hospital gurney;
From landing pad to the ER was a short journey.
They put the oxygen mask on my face,
Traveling down that swirling Tunnel Of Doom,
I awoke the next morning and discovered
I was sharing a sunny room
With three other recovering guys.
Clean, fresh-smelling white sheets!
It was a most pleasurable, pleasant surprise.

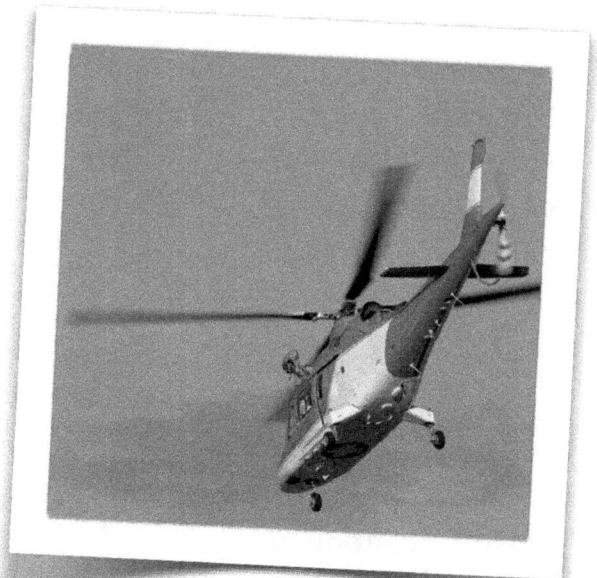

11 RECOVERY AND RECUPERATION

I was starving to death,
And it was almost noon.
The Japanese-American Doctor,
He was a very good Dude,
So very righteously cool!

He told me how incredibly lucky
I was to still be here;
The Shark's teeth had just missed,
All of the arteries inside of my wrist.
And now my hand was sewn up,
In a permanent fist;
Until the skin could grow back,
Was the gist of the fix.
Otherwise, if his razor sharp teeth,
Had not just missed my arteries,
I would have had more than plenty to fear;
I would have quickly bled out like a deer.

Even if I had survived,
My hand certainly would have not;
For me it was incredibly lucky
That only my pinkie-finger tendon
Was the only thing, internally,
That had been completely severed.
To close up my arm, externally,
It took exactly 46 stitches;
And they kept me heavily loaded up
With lots of strong antibiotics.

The Doctor said,

"Staying hospitalized for two weeks is a must.

Since you have been on such a low-calorie diet,

You're going to have to double your meal intake, I trust."

The Doctor also expressed

That the local TV News,

Was waiting patiently for interviews.

He also said that the Island Police,

Were determined to interrogate me.

The Cops alleged that I had sustained knife wounds;

They wanted to pull a raid on the poor Jesus Freaks.

I categorically denied any talk of it at all.

I held out my forearm,

Removing the bandage, so they could see it all.

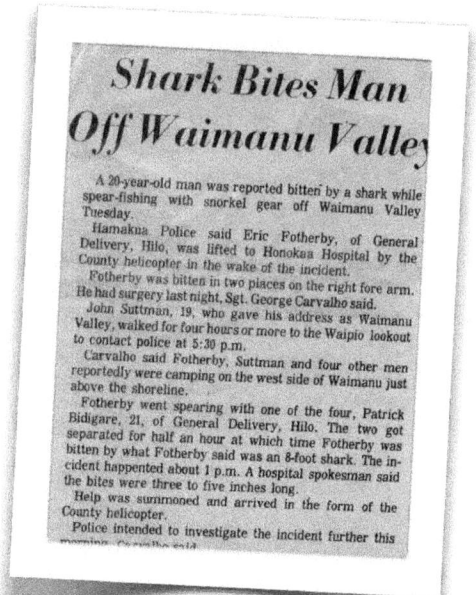

Shark Bites Man Off Waimanu Valley

A 20-year-old man was reported bitten by a shark while spear-fishing with snorkel gear off Waimanu Valley Tuesday.

Hamakua Police said Eric Fotherby, of General Delivery, Hilo, was lifted to Honokaa Hospital by the County helicopter in the wake of the incident.

Fotherby was bitten in two places on the right fore arm. He had surgery last night, Sgt. George Carvalho said.

John Suttman, 19, who gave his address as Waimanu Valley, walked for four hours or more to the Waipio lookout to contact police at 5:30 p.m.

Carvalho said Fotherby, Suttman and four other men reportedly were camping on the west side of Waimanu just above the shoreline.

Fotherby went spearing with one of the four, Patrick Bidigare, 21, of General Delivery, Hilo. The two got separated for half an hour at which time Fotherby was bitten by what Fotherby said was an 8-foot shark. The incident happented about 1 p.m. A hospital spokesman said the bites were three to five inches long.

Help was summoned and arrived in the form of the County helicopter.

Police intended to investigate the incident further this morning, Carvalho said.

"Take a look at my arm,
Still oozing fishbone-infected purulence,
My arm is still leaking supporting evidence!"

Luckily one of the Cops was the cousin,
Of my girlfriend Maile.
Whom I had met on the plane;
We had dated in the previous weeks.
After talking to Maile,
He then vouched for me.

I had to turn down the TV News Team,
Because the Cops in Kona, it seemed,
Might still be looking for Slick,
Who had two weeks previously
Been apprehended by some hotel staff,
For stealing a gallon of cottage cheese,
One night sneaking around a hotel kitchen.
The staff had to release him on his honor;
Of course he had promised to turn himself in.

My protective Doctor assured the Police,
That my cuts were sustained,
By Very Large Shark's Teeth.
So Slick went on back to Hilo,
And I settled into the Hospital,
For the next two lazy weeks.
I got to know two delightful roommates,
But the third guy was almost always asleep.

The tall one was a long-faced,

One hundred percent
Full-blooded Hawai'ian guy.
He was dying of cancer,
And he had come from the Island of Lanai.

Whenever he had visitations
From any of his family and friends,
He loved to have me
Tell My Shark Story,
Over and over again.
He said that before World War II,
Hawai'i had been truly,
A God-Given Paradise.

The other guy had a leg problem;
He was a Filipino-American,
And also a corporate security guard.
His Wife and his loving Family
Were so genuinely very friendly,
Brought in lots of Lumpia,
And Adobo Chicken And Beef;
Always a delicious buffet on our ward!
The time passed very quickly;
I healed and mended very swiftly.

Hitchhiking with only one usable arm,
I was now so looking forward
To seeing all of the gang back at Hilo,
To lots of beer and smoking Pakalolo.

Before long I was once again hitching,
In the heavy, drenching, pouring rain,
With my unwieldy 70-pound backpack;
My back and arms were feeling the pain.

I was attempting to return very fleetly,
I was planning to show up discreetly
To observe why Slick didn't meet me.
It was my homecoming comeback,
I had now boomeranged right on back,
To that friendly, familiar pizza shack!

12 HILO AGAIN, WITH SHOCKING SEISMIC CONFESSIONS

I arrived back in Hilo,
On another of those dark, rainy nights;
It was so refreshing to find cover,
Under the bright, Edison-Bulb Lights.
I found Slick drinking a beer,
Enjoying a fest and a jest;
Tree climbing was what he did best.
Lack of fear and unlimited strength,
Arboreal climbing is the test;
That is what it takes
To reach the Eagle's Nest

His other talent, his greatest skill yet,
Came in a very close, second best:
Affable and extremely fascinating,
Casual and completely captivating,
He had a knack for engaging
A lot of very attractive young ladies.

But alas, poor Slick was so Dedicated
To his only True Love, way back home,
Where she lived with unyielding parents,
Back in glamorous San Francisco.
And like Rapunzel, who couldn't escape.
Slick was restricted from visiting,
Wholly prohibited, legally restrained.

She went by the name of Jane.
Her Father was a Judge

Who really hated Slick's guts;
Which constantly made him feel ashamed.

So in Hawai'i, when Slick had seduced
Another attractive young girl
Into moving on towards the hay,
He was unable to go All The Way;
He couldn't go through with it,
I guess you could say.
To her he would sadly confess,
Overwhelmed with despair and sorrow,
He said his heart was an emotional mess,
He was still devoted to another.
"But I would like to introduce you
To my good-looking 'brother'!"

He would forget about using the Buddy System
When diving in the ocean together,
And he forgot me again at Honoka'a,
The exit day of my hospital stay.
But you see why it was the good-natured Slick,
That I always kept as my really good buddy.
He was the finest Wing Man one could possibly be;
He just kept introducing adorable girls to me.

All of the girls flew over and stuck to him,
He was like soft, sticky flypaper;
That is why I also stuck with him, too.
He was the one that I always kept True Blue.
Give me a break, wouldn't you, too?

388

One day we were cruising around town,
In a new Volkswagen Bug;
This good-looking Babe
Freely loaned it to Slick,
For just a kiss and a hug.
It had a full-blown stereo
And we would park at the beach,
Listening to our favorite band —
Grand Funk Railroad —
Playing "Gimme' Shelter"
That Vietnam song,
Over and over again,
All afternoon long.
Blasting the volume,
Drinking beer, joshing and joking,
Nimbly rolling, breezily toking,
Hawai'i's Major League Pakalolo, so bold;
Famously called Kona Gold.

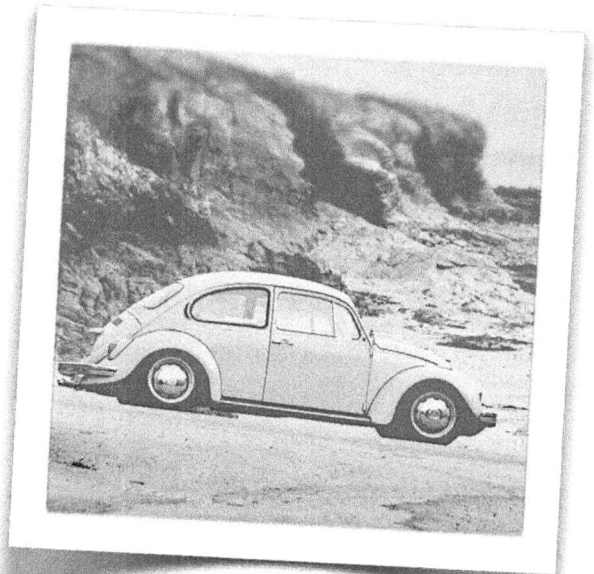

While casually observing
The splendiferous Wahinis,
Happily swimming and surfing,
In their teeny, tiny bikinis.

Back to business,
We went scouting around
For a new-to-us, slightly-used,
Condemned Home to anoint
As our new Hippie Joint.
In this very cool little town.
We found a terrific new place,
And all that was needed,
Was a rug for this space.
But that night at our palace,
We were soon to discover
We were no longer alone;
Someone else had arrived at our home!

We found out that
Those boys from Ohio
Had also just previously,
Moved in from the wild;
And now we were sharing
Our brand-new domicile.
It was all fun and games,
We were having good times,
Relating to each other,
Sharing our dives and our climbs.

Suddenly angry Pele's Volcano

Rumbled and grumbled and quaked!
Out of the windows and doors,
We jumped and we tumbled!
Once again, Mother Nature
Had us respectfully humbled.

Having shared one more scary,
Adventurous time together,
The Ohio boys decided to disburden.
They thought that it would be best,
They had something very serious,
That they wanted to confess;
To jettison some of their guilt
Easily removed off of their chests.

Up until now,
They could not decide,
Whether or not they should tell me,

That they had a lot of remorse to confide.

During our time together
In the beautiful Waipi'o Valley,
It seems they had washed the meat,
Of that bloody pig carcass right in the sea;
Instead of washing the blood off in the sand,
By using buckets of water on the land.
Stupidly they were spreading
Mammalian blood out in the sea,
That is why a Hungry Shark came looking for me!

And up until now,
They had been
Somewhat frightened of me,
Too timid to confess their offense;
Confess and set themselves free.
What could I say?
How else could I reply?
"Sure, good buddies, don't worry about it."
I said I was letting it go as I told them,
"Oh what the Hell!"

I would like to thank my Dear God,
That I had had such Extremely Good Luck,
And didn't end up, as a Tasty Shark Lunch.
But if it weren't for the Ohio Boy's Magnum,
That was stashed somewhere unknown,
That "Good Buddy" would have gotten
A very swift, left-handed,
Punch in the nose!

392

Back at the pizza place,
I suggested the next day,
That the timing seemed right
For us to go travel to some new place.
So let's not delay!
We've got only three more weeks
For our trip, left to stay.

I could not swim in the water,
Because my wounds still had to stay dry;
Scabs had not yet congealed,
They were insufficiently healed.
I was thinking that we needed a change.
It seemed like a good time
To travel to the island next door:
Find a new scene,
Try some of that new herbal green,
Smoke some of that Maui Wowie!

13 ON TO MAUI

Leaving the Big Island,
Slick and I took Hawai'ian Airlines' Island Hopper;
Coming in for a landing
Was quite a show stopper.
When the pilot was banking
Into his left turn,
The tip of our plane's wing
Almost dipped in the surf!
A downward draft
Nearly cart-wheeled us
Right into the turf!

Arriving at the Kahului Airport,
We were not sure where to go;
Didn't have a clue of what to do.
A friendly Haole at the airport said,
"Baldwin Beach Park is pretty cool."

So we moseyed on down the road, not too far;
On the way, we stopped at the market,
And we picked up some food for the park.
Soon after, we met a bunch of friendly,
Ex-Vietnam-Veteran-Dudes,
Who welcomed us with open arms,
To join on in with their Brood.

But first we had to go look and see
The most popular Lahaina Beach;
We heard it was definitely more

For the Mainland's Nouveau Riche.
There were many expensive high-rise hotels,
Innumerable airport buses always unloading,
Endless lines of little blue-haired old ladies;
The scene gave us a fearful future foreboding.
So we hitchhiked right on back,
To our new-found communal pad
With the Veteran Military Elite,
Back to beautiful Baldwin Beach.

Somehow, once again,
Slick had managed to pick up
Another lonely, gorgeous girl.
And yet again, he held true to his Love,
Who was waiting for him back home,
Locked up high in a tower,
By the evil, wicked Judge.

Slick brought this new girl down to the beach,
And introduced her to me, you see;
This Haole girl, fresh from the airport,
Jumped right into the sleeping bag with me!
Those were the days of the Hippies,
When lots of Good Lovin' was free.

We all went hitchhiking out to Hana,
To a place called The Seven Sacred Pools,
Somehow we managed to pick up,
Two interlopers, who joined us, too.

We hiked on up above the shimmering pools,

Made camp with a small fire in a clean, dry cave;
But I woke up in the middle of the night to find
My new girlfriend was on top of this guy,
She was making love to this Vagabond Fool.
I thought "Well, Hell,
That is not very cool!"

In the morning Slick and I broke camp,
And with a wave I said goodbye.
She begged me not to leave her,
With these two loser, goofy guys.
I said, "You should have considered your plight,
Before you started screwing around last night."

So we were contented to leave Hana,
With all of its mythology, so ominous.
I applauded my new unattached position;
After only three days
She had quickly become
Way too much of a burden;
I was very happy once again to be free.
Although she was very cute and pretty;
And I accede she had a very voluptuous body,
Regrettably, that girl was far too nutty for me!

Back at Baldwin Beach,
I still couldn't swim, surf or dive.
My arm was still leaking and seeping,
A staph infection could get in and thrive.
At night on the beach, I was sleeping;
All day, I was just hanging out with the guys.

I met this permanently-wounded Marine
Who went by the name of Mark.
He loaned me a new best-seller book,
That was called "Chariots of the Gods."
I read his books and we played chess together,
Enjoyed lazy afternoons convalescing in the park.

His right leg was thickly scarred,
Heavily disfigured from shrapnel,
And he had the same scars
On his damaged right arm;
He had been a military advisor,
Up in the mountains of Vietnam.

In the morning, all of the guys
Would walk down the beach road
To Paia, to an old drugstore soda fountain,
Owned by two lesbians, I was told.

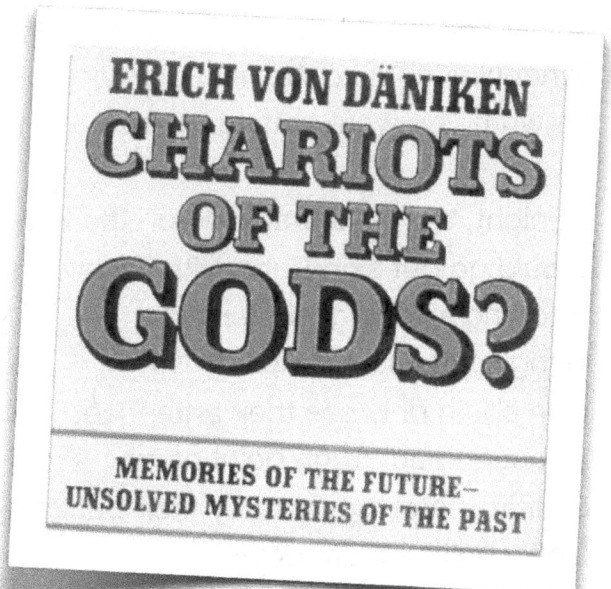

ERICH VON DÄNIKEN

CHARIOTS OF THE GODS?

MEMORIES OF THE FUTURE—
UNSOLVED MYSTERIES OF THE PAST

They made the greatest of omelets,
For only a pittance; I was sold!
Then we would mosey on over
To a two-table pool hall;
And for just one thin dime,
This friendly, old Chinese guy
Would rack up the balls.

Later we would saunter on over
To the bar in the late afternoon;
For an ice cold, long-necked beer,
And a free platter of pu pus.
Sometimes it was fried dolphin,
Or hot dog pieces wrapped in bacon.
Peace, passion and pleasure in Paradise;
It was all right here for the taking.

Every day was something different,
A surprise you just never could quite know,
What was coming the next day for dinner,
Or what you were getting to chew with your brew.

At night, the guys that lived on the beach
Would go out skindiving with flashlights.
Spotting sleeping lobsters,
Hanging in fissures upside down,
One could only see their antennae,
Appearing out front, pointing up.
Swiftly snatching them by their backs,
Deftly pulling them down,
Then forcing them into the game bag.

We would barbecue fifteen or twenty,
Our gorging going on late into the night!

Every single night at midnight
A Samoan Security Watchman,
Who was good buddies with the Vets,
Would always appear with a cold case of Primo beer.
Which he traded for the crustaceans' cavity shells.
With his fingers digging the goo out of their bodies,
Sucking on shells and slurping up all of the guts,
It was his most personal delight, you could tell!

Slick decided to hike Haleakala Crater,
With some of the guys from the beach.
I was extremely disappointed,
Because I was unable to go, with bad feet;
Because of staph infections on my foot,
I was completely unable to put on my boots!

If you want to cool down from the heat,
And you swim in the ocean with open cuts,
You'll get pus-infected scabs that won't heal;
Without antibiotics, the wounds won't congeal.

That is something
The Hawai'ian Tourist Bureau
Always fails to mention,
When you happily buy your plane tickets,
And make your hotel reservations,
For your Tropical Paradise Vacation.

The Tourist Bureau never will warn you,
About the many spiny Sea Urchins
That will surely poison your blood;
The Moray Eels with razor-sharp teeth,
And the Sharks that consider you Food!
And an island of Locals,
Who want you off of their beach,
Long gone, forever, for good!

14 SKULL SECURITY COMPANY

I had this old human skull —
A present from the beach guys —
That had been happily given to me.
It was from a local graveyard
That was being reclaimed
By the incoming surf on the beach.
They had found the large skull,
Half-exposed in the sand,
By the waves, at the edge of the sea.
They began having fears of paranormal possession;
They were experiencing Hawai'ian superstitions,
So they decided to give it to me.

I would place it on top of my gear
Facing the flap, from inside of the tent.
When thieves would sneak in,
The first thing they would see,

Was one of their less-fortunate kin;
A clean, naked skull,
Staring most hauntingly,
Piercingly, fierce back at them!

I met this handsome Hawai'ian guy,
Who also went by the name of Slick,
He had come there looking for me;
Firsthand, he wanted to hear My Story,
And observe closely the scars on my arm,
He had a personal curiosity!
Like everyone else, he had cause for alarm.

Every morning he would swim,
Three miles up and down the beach.
With his finely-trimmed mustache,
He looked very much like
A famous, old-time, silent-movie star,
The popular Douglas Fairbanks, Jr.

He introduced me to Sashimi
With soy sauce and hot mustard.
For a homophobic, straight guy, I had to admit,
He really had me quite charmed.

He said he could free dive
Down to 90 feet deep.
I was extremely impressed:
Even wearing scuba fins,
I could only reach 50 feet.

He had just quit his job,
At Sea World, over on Waikiki Beach,
Where he had to free up a stuck gate,
At 70 feet deep.
With a Killer Whale at his back,
He was within easy reach.
He said, that just like me,
His experience
Had shaken him to his Core;
And like me,
He was reconsidering,
Whether it was worth it,
To go on back for more.

Then this Portuguese EMT,
A Local Ex-Vietnam-Veteran Medic,
He came searching me out,
He wanted to see for himself;
Word of my skull had been traveling about.
He said that what I was doing,
Was extremely distasteful at best.
I had been using that old cranium
Like a junkyard guard dog;
It was my personal security system
Exploiting the Locals' superstitions.

He said that he had a solution that was creative.
He had a large medical collection,
It was a shelf full of skulls back at home,
He wanted to add my bony pal
To his home-based congregation,

Where it would never again be alone.
So I gave it up to my new friend,
And as yet, please understand,
It was purely the most ignorant move,
That I have ever knowingly agreed to.
I was aware of the most likely outcome,
But my fear of him calling the Cops,
Was the reason for a decision so dumb!
Without the protection of the skull,
It took only two days
For the Locals to clean out all of my stuff.
At that point, I was more than ready to give in;
I had just about had enough.

I now considered these Locals,
As pernicious people, quite wicked.
Besides my backpack and food,
They stole my return-home plane ticket!
The Airlines made me wait for two weeks,
For them to re-issue, it was by far the quickest.

All I had left were my flip-flops,
A T-shirt, and some shorts.
That was it!
Registering in time for college,
It was turning out to be an abort.

Luckily I had the serial numbers
To a couple of Traveler's Cheques,
To use for beer and delicious pu pus,
Plus Spam-and-chicken omelets.

I slept like a crab on the beach,
Two weeks, without any blanket!

Finally we were going to be able,
To get on a plane going back home.
We had almost half of a new 747
Much to ourselves, with free movies,
Lots of snacks, and alcoholic drinks.

Washing up, with wild hair to comb,
All over the plane we roamed,
Like a couple of mischievous elves,
Flirting with the young stewardesses,
Telling them we wanted their kisses!

We were heading back to our circle of friends,
No more loneliness, or always feeling alone;
Cheerfully returning to Northern California,
It felt so good to be soon coming back home!

RUNNING OFF TO AMSTERDAM

1 ASCHAFFENBURG, GERMANY

Back in May of 1988,
My Mother had decided
That we now had a date.
She was taking me back to Germany
For all of our relatives to meet and see.
Thirty-eight years old, I was now a week-end Dad,
I was happily divorced and once-again single,
With a Son, seven years old, who also had a Step-Dad;
I was ready to go out in the world and mingle.

We flew into Frankfurt Airport,
Something unusual to report:
I was notably shocked to see
Two-man teams of Combat Military
Packing 9mm machine guns,
While carefully eyeballing everyone.

The 1972 Munich Olympic Massacre
Had undeniably created such a stir,
That even 17 years later,
They were still needed to deter,
Muslim Slimeballs creating Fear;
Maniacal Scumbags trying to create Terror.

At the airport we rented an Opel Kadett,
It took us three laps just to find the exit.
The airport was under a massive reconstruction,

It was difficult at first, just to drive and to function.
The street signs of course, were only in German;
I was giving up, they were just too hard to read.
I then began focusing all of my attention,
To only the International signs that I would need.
Perusing the map in anticipation,
I started driving on pure instinct,
Trusting only in compass direction,
Ancient winding roads, so indistinct.
Without anyone navigating,
It was incredibly frustrating!

My Mother was extremely lucky
That she had not been very hungry;
She had given her sandwich to me,
Expired Leftovers, unbeknownst I did eat.

Two tainted sandwiches of roast beef,
From the last flight, served on our plane,

Were causing me dire Intestinal Grief.
My bowels were about to explode,
It was only about ten kilometers to go;
I was desperate to get on the commode!

Wending our way to Aschaffenburg,
A quaint little historical town,
To find my Auntie's apartment,
"Thank the Lord!" that soon it was found.
Dashing up the stairs in her lobby,
I ran into her bathroom to purge,
Where I spent a couple of hours,
Regurgitating with a surge.
Swallowing a whole lot of water,
More than I could possibly drink,
Exhausted, drained, and I stink.

My insides had been churning,
Like bad wine, it was turning,
My bowels were acidic and sour;
I was morose, distressed, feeling dour.

When my Mother was only four years old,
My Grandfather was offered a high-paying job.
He left Henry Ford's Plant in Detroit City,
To help support Panzer Tank manufacturing.
They went by Steamship, way back in 1933,
As yet still unawares of Hitler's insanity.

My Mother had an idyllic German childhood.
Music and hiking, festive holiday celebrations;

She had no idea of the fear now gripping the nation.
The Allied Bombers started flying overhead,
She was bombed out of three different homes.
She was so incredibly lucky,
That she was not found injured or dead.

But now to my chagrin, most unfortunately,
Pronouncing the German vocabulary —
Even if I could remember the terminology —
The language was way too difficult for me.
Socializing and visiting many of our relatives,
As I was unable to understand German,
I may as well been deaf or uncommunicative;
In Europe, if you are not multi-lingual,
No one feels obligated to be commiserative.

2 KRONBERG, GERMANY

I went to visit an old High School friend,
Who was teaching in Kronberg,
At the International School,
Where my Aunt had been teaching, too.
He took me to the Badhaus,
Full of nude men and women,
Who were exercising and swimming.
It was Nirvana for Pervs;
I was enthusiastically brimming,
Viewing all of those beautiful women.

Then we left and he bought some flowers,
We were going to visit his middle-aged "friend."
I found bringing flowers to be a bit weird,
Actually I did make a protest in the end.

But I really did not want to interfere.
He said it was normal, that he was just "being;"
That he was just acting like a normal European.
Exactly what kind of relationship,
That he privately had with his "friend,"
Only now was really, just beginning to sink in.

They set me up with this thirtyish beautiful blond.
But even after three days with her as my escort,
Using all of my charms, I was still terribly frustrated;
I was totally unable to seduce her, I must report.

I dejectedly realized then,

That I had been deftly conned.
That she was just a distraction,
This very attractive Lesbian.

All of that time, spent on wasted endeavor;
They thought that they were being very clever.
She had just been putting me on
So I would not notice my buddy,
His old boyfriend, quite a bit chubby.
What in the closet, was really going on?

I thought of my friend's Wife and his Kid,
All the way back home in Michigan;
And if he considered what he did,
As a Catholic, was he living in Super Sin?

His boyfriend had given me my first Pot taste,
For the first time in two weeks.
He was stingy, selfishly sharing so little,
It was frustrating, almost a total waste.
Smoking my favorite Evil Weed
He teased my desire, my need.
He acted like his Pot was made of Gold.
If not for the respect of my old school friend,
This bearded, sausage-fat German,
He, instead of the marijuana,
Would have quickly been rolled!
In Germany, because Weed was so rare,
He used it like a carrot on a stick,
Only to tempt, offered very little to share,
A very small sample indeed, what a Prick!

In Deutschland it was very risky to get stoned.
Because of uncompromising German authorities,
The German Polizie liked to work hand-in-hand
With the Anal American Military;
I heard they liked to go nuts in regards to drugs.

When it came to Pot,
They were still a bunch
Of European Rednecks
That detested marijuana,
Whether we liked it or not!

I returned back to Aschaffenburg,
Did a few trips with my Mom and my Aunt,
But I was beginning to have that Urge,
That no amount of alcohol
Was able to discourage.

3 AMSTERDAM, THE NETHERLANDS

I told them that I had made some new plans,
And that I was running off to Amsterdam.
I bought a round-trip train ticket
To this Very Liberal Dutch Destination,
Where I had recently made
My week-long hotel reservation,
Right directly across the street
From the downtown train station.

Riding the train towards Cologne,
I met many American college-aged girls.
Another new country every couple of days;
Their traveling style was a maniacal blur —
A mindless, obsessed, reeling whirl.
They visited the House of Anne Frank,
Saw the famous sights of Amsterdam,

Would view a few Dutch paintings;
Back on the train, hurriedly scram.
Their excursion was a bit of a sham!

Documenting their presence
With photos, so picturesque.
To authenticate to everyone —
Friends and relatives back home —
That they actually had been there,
That they knew how to really roam.

Sending proof to everyone,
That they were not terrified
Of traveling far and wide;
Doing it on their own, all alone.
Get the most bang for your buck,
Out on the road, pushing your luck.
Wringing out much value to spare,
From that exorbitantly-priced plane fare.
Then prancing on to Paris, France;
It was a race, leaving nothing to chance.
From the rain on the plain in Spain,
Then moving onto England's trains.

If it was located in the travel brochure,
They definitely planned on going there.
A most ridiculous Continental Dance,
Spread out all over, such a great expanse.

We stopped at Cologne.
This well-dressed black man
414

Got on the train all alone;
He was also going to Amsterdam.
He decided to sit down next to me,
Because I looked American,
Much too obviously.

He had been an Army Lieutenant,
Managing a large office, all full
Of young stenographic women;
He said that his life was never dull.

Germany had offered him a career
When he left the U.S. Military,
A Mercedes sports car to steer,
Lots of excellent German beer.
Nary, not a bit of racism;
Quite to the contrary.

But if he wanted recreational drugs,
One had to go and then deal with the thugs;
Living in alleys, always trying to scam,
Roaming the streets of Amsterdam.
He suggested that when our train ride ends,
That we hang out together, get high and be friends.

When I arrived,
I checked into my clean Dutch hotel
They charged about forty dollars a night.
The Ex-Army Lieutenant
Wended his way down to the canal boats;
He got a berth on the boat for only ten bucks.

It was managed by only one horny Frenchman,
Using lonely women who were down on their luck,
Not only for sex, but also cooking and cleaning up.

It came with a breakfast, advertised as 'American.'
Cooked by innocent women, destitute, bankrupt.
These Cowgirls recently ingrained to Cocaine,
Who had spent all of their money on drugs;
They only had sex left to trade.
(Better with the Frenchman
Then the criminal street thugs.)

Here in Amsterdam
They now found themselves stranded;
Without cash for anything,
Which survival demanded.

In exchange for handing out flyers all day
In front of the train station,
And for some fellatio and some sex,
The Frenchman would only pay for
Their bed, and an American breakfast.

The Ex-Lieutenant and I went out in the streets,
Seeing if we could find a successful drug meet.
It didn't take us very long,
To be surrounded by a throng,
Of Cokeheads and Junkies,
A bunch of Losers and Flunkies.

But they had no wares to display.
416

They wanted to bring us samples,
I said I was not at all interested,
After the drugs have been stepped on.
"I've got a hundred dollars to spend,
I want to meet your guy in the end."
Meanwhile my Ex-Lieutenant friend,
Went and ran off to get some heroin.

Suddenly this huge African guy showed up.
I am six foot four and he had two inches on me;
Outweighed me by more than one hundred pounds,
His musculature was very impressive, visually.
In West Africa he was a tribal chief,
Where he would spend six months of the year,
Living like the King he was obviously born to be;
He had multiple wives, so many children to rear.
Then for the other six months,
In the beautiful city of Amsterdam,

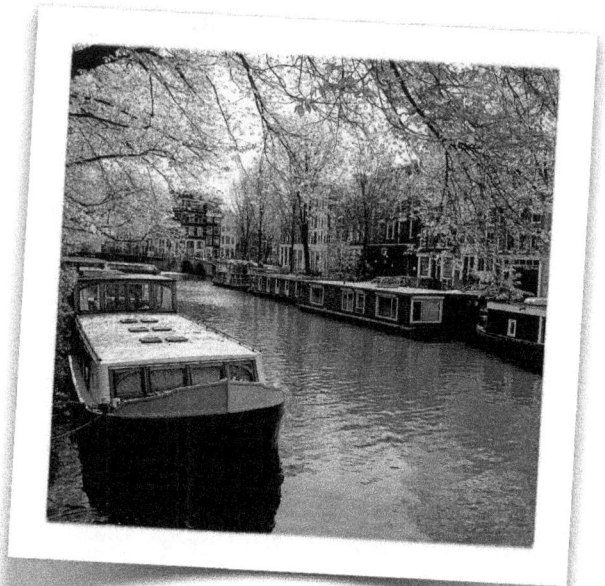

He would deal drugs.
His cocaine was very good,
And it didn't take much;
My resistance was such,
That I really couldn't do much.

He asked me to come and join him
On his illicit delivery rounds.
I had done some Karate,
Some tournament fighting,
Back in the day,
When I was in college.
So I thought I could handle myself,
If it came to a little street fighting.

So off I went blindly,
With this big African stud,
Into this Middle-Eastern ghetto,
With dangerous desert Gorillas,
Dealing with Islamic thugs!

He had me stand away,
A few doors down,
And across the street;
Just hangin' around.

When out of the cracks in the wall
Appeared two greasy Arab Assassins
With their long knives exposed;
A most desperate situation.
They were heading my way;

I yelled out just one word: "Hey!"

Then that African guy shot them one look,
Immediately they stopped in their tracks,
And then they sleazily faded away;
He instantaneously had aborted their attack.
I told the African that he must be
One Bad-Ass Motherfucker!
Then he smiled and said to me,
"I do okay, they are afraid of me."

I returned back to the canal boat
To look for my Army Ex-Lieutenant,
But he was not anywhere around.
His ghetto blaster I had found;
I plugged it in, then it exploded!
Then it smoked and it burned.
I had been warned about the high voltage in Europe;
But because of the unusual outlet plugs,
I thought that this canal boat
Had already been electrically converted.

The Army Ex-Lieutenant then returned;
He couldn't be conciliated or mollified.
I gave him my 90 dollars worth of cocaine.
He was now pacified; we were good friends again.

I walked a few blocks on down the way,
To that fabled and famous coffee shop
That sold hash and sold pot;
Everyone knew it as The Bulldog Cafe.

There was a big chalkboard menu
Behind the Barista's cash register;
Many exotic varieties to choose.
It was such bliss and exuberance,
No fear, not feeling paranoid,
No longer an outlaw or a gangster.
Decidedly an unadulterated pleasure,
An enthusiastically-enjoyed treasure.
It was truly a genuine luxury,
For this apprehensive American guy,
Just to go out and get high,
Exposed, uncaring in the public eye.

I had a problem with their hash;
It was so heavily opiated,
That after only three puffs,
It would make me nod off and crash.

I hastily had to find my hotel bed;
Spent more than three hours,
Sleeping it off instead.
So then I went out on the streets again,
To find my big African friend.
I needed to buy some more cocaine,
So I could smoke this great hash
Without rapidly having to crash.

I went to check on my ex-Lieutenant friend;
In the middle of the day he was passed out again.
He wanted some cocaine to wake up,
He wanted to trade my white for his brown.
He talked me into snorting some down —
Two teeny, tiny lines of heroin.
It was really no big deal,
I did not feel anything.

After dark I went on out to the disco.
My sinuses dislodged,
And I swallowed my phlegm;
It wasn't too long
Before I hardly could stand.
Overwhelmed, I knew that I was overdosing;
I had to stay on my feet, and just keep on going.

I stumbled outside to walk it off.
To do drugs in Amsterdam was not a crime,
But if you passed out on the sidewalk,
You were going to jail, to do some time.
That was the least of my worries;

Right about then I was more fearful of dying.
I kept walking alongside of the building,
Occasionally leaning against it with one arm.
I did that for about two or three hours,
Until I got back some bodily control.
Then I walked gently back to my room
And took a moderately cold shower.

Back in my teens in San Francisco,
I had done some chipping, with a needle.
I had almost died from Hepatitis,
So I had some experience with uncontrolled reeling;
I had to stay on my feet and fight this.
Keep my life from slipping and sliding away!
I knew what I had been feeling.
But I made it back to my hotel bed,
Where I gratefully rested my tired head.

Later on the next morning,
I went down to the canal boat
To check on the Army Ex-Lieutenant.
He had disappeared, mysteriously gone.
No one seemed to be distressed;
Where he had disappeared to,
It was anybody's guess!

I went to the bar on the canal boat,
To buy an American breakfast.
I already had drank my two Coffee Nudges,
From the bartender at the bar across the square,
Who made them for me; my recipe I had shared.
It cost me only three Guilders;
The same as a buck.
Feeling somewhat perplexed,
Wishing for good luck
With women and drugs.

I was trying to decide
What I was going to do next.
Currently I was enjoying the scenery:
Watching the ferry disembarking
Fifteen busty, blond Swedish sightseers.

Then up walked this sexy, Sicilian-American girl,
Who had spent last night with the Frenchman.
Her face was only a 4 or a 5,
But her body was most definitely a 10.
I told her that I would share my cocaine,
If she would just show me around;

See some of the sights in this town.

So together we set off on our merry jaunt;
We went to all of the shops and outdoor cafes.
While at the bistros enjoying the ambiance,
We were having a very enjoyable day!
Until, like a slap, striking my shoulder,
Abruptly I was unceremoniously hit,
With what seemed like about a quarter of a cup,
Of very white, gooey and slimy,
Especially-disgusting seagull shit!

The waiter absolutely refused
To loan me his precious bar towel;
But assured me it was good luck
To be crapped on by scavenger fowl!

So I walked right inside of the bistro,
I said, "You had better clean off my shoulder,
Otherwise, I will stand and refuse to go,
As we all hang around here, getting older."

Finally they gave up the quarrel,
The run-in, the ruckus, the row,
For such an incredibly-valuable towel,
Finally, ungraciously bestowed.

There were multitudinous new fashions
At innumerable stores on display.
There were many fashionable
Real-leather handmade boots from Spain,

For which they were only asking
Just 40 dollars; it was a small price to pay.

In New York City, where my new companion
Had been applying makeup on models all day,
Those boots went for a minimum of at least,
The tidy sum of one hundred and twenty dollars;
It was exactly three times the price to pay.
Amsterdam and Hong Kong
Were the only two International cities
With no importation taxes to be applied.
Everything was extremely cheap to buy!

She said, "I have something to show you,
Something else that I almost forgot."
She took me down to the canal,
Along the water by the riverfront,
To a canal boat that was docked
Downtown, across from the train station.
She took me aboard, she had passenger status.
There were a few Dutchmen and many Jamaicans,
Some Muslim Malaccans, and also some Haitians.
It was set up like a Sunday Church Bazaar,
A stateroom with a square of rectangular tables.
But instead of selling baked goods and ice cream bars,
There were cash registers, scales,
Plastic bags of powders without labels.
A cacophony of voices,
Shouting louder and louder.
With eight-inch-high piles
Of white and brown powders.

Just breathing the filmy dust in the air,
Made me feel like I could dance
Like the debonair Fred Astaire.
So I stepped outside on the deck;
I had to get a bit of fresh air.

I saw this 14-year-old Dutch kid
Lying back on a pile of ropes,
With a syringe hanging out of his arm,
Passed out, all loaded with dope.
I could only shake my head,
Because it wouldn't be long,
Before that kid ended up dead.

This short, stocky Congo-looking guy
Was trying to appear menacing;
Giving me the "stink eye."
He thought he was threatening,
With one of those little bent-tipped,
Red-handled paring knives.
I said, "If you come any closer,
We are going to find out,
When we hit the cold water,
How good you are able to swim!"
He looked at the brown, dirty flotsam,
As he contemplated my sneering, confident grin.
Suddenly he turned, and took off like the wind.

We walked around sightseeing
For the rest of the week.
Then she made me an offer

That surely made me think.
She had two older sisters
Who were married to Mobsters.
One had a mansion in London, and a villa in Spain,
The other had a mansion in Paris and a villa in Greece;
We could stay in either, just as long as we pleased.
They were usually vacant,
The owners were distant.
But I had a Government Job,
And a seven-year-old Boy;
To avoid a custody battle,
I needed to return back to Seattle.
Famous for the bluest of skies
A great place for outdoorsy guys!
But I was not really yet ready
To throw my cares to the wind;
To put all of my trust,
In a Gangster-Connected Cokehead.

If I were to trust my recently-found friend,
There were many possible scenarios
On how to end up irrefutably dead!
So, at the end of the week we said, "Ciao,"
And I got back on the train thinking, "Wow."

4 BACK TO GERMANY, THEN AUSTRIA, THEN HOME

Just as the train crossed the border into Germany,
The Polizei were searching freely and thoroughly;
Fierce-looking German Shepherds, sniffing intensely.
Sitting in my captain-sized seat,
I was shocked, scared and appalled —
They let their dog stick his nose into
And also shove it under my balls.

I am glad I had been smart enough
Not to bring any stash back.
"Do not try to act tough,"
The Ex-Lieutenant had said,
"Hey Guy, do not mess with the Polizei!"

"They have wicked billy clubs
With vibrating, spring-loaded pistons,
That quickly close up the distance,
To impact and tear off your face.
If you resist in the least, or defy,
You get the Nine-Millimeter spray;
No qualms about watching you die."

I made it back to Aschaffenburg.
After hanging around the Marktplatz,
I loaded up my Mom and my Aunt,
Back on the Autobahn again, in the Opel Kadett.

I had been anticipating this,
Getting ready for some fast-driving bliss,

My foot heavy on the pedal to the metal.
My shoe flat on the floor, the concrete, devoured;
Almost 188 kilometers per hour,
Essentially 112 miles an hour!
To get out of the slow lane, I barely had enough power.

Do not even think about driving the Autobahn's fast lane,
Unless your car is fast enough to do more
Than 228 kilometers per hour,
(To you, about 137.5 miles per hour);
At that speed, you had better know how to drive!

We were going to visit
My Uncle Hermann, the German,
Way down south in Munich;
He was one Hell of a good guy!
He drove us up to Salzburg,
To enjoy a little Austrian culture.

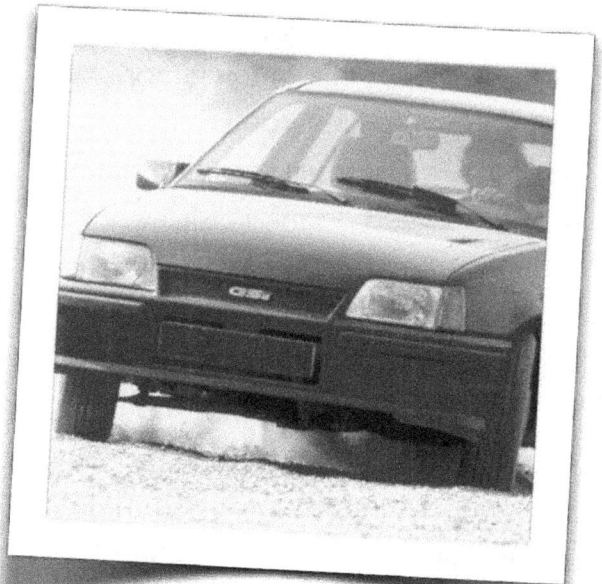

We toured the BMW factory,
Then we went out for a drive.
It is Mozart's birth home;
A very musical departure,
Around town which to roam.

Then he took us to the city of Passau,
At the convergence of three rivers,
And three countries that surround.
This was where Napoleon
Had set up his headquarters.
The Imperial French Army
Was marching to Russia;
This was the place from where
They would be getting their orders.

Paris' Arc de Triomphe
Had been commissioned
By Napoleon in 1806,
To memorialize his many victories.
But in the end, the irony,
It recorded the heartbreaking history,
Of all the dead generals
From The Grande Arme´e March;
Not a triumph, but a grim tragedy.
It was a Hellish story of bitter winter cold,
In the unusually frigid winter of 1812.
He lost more than 600,000 men all told,
That was the number of men that were felled.
It is the story of how he did send,
So many men to such a disastrous end.

430

The Arc de Triomphe has evolved
Into a prodigious gravestone of death.

Passau was where we ended our trip,
No more energy left to cavort around.
Back to Hermann's hometown of Dingelfing,
Then sadly we said, "Auf Wiedersehen."
Dejectedly we headed on back,
To the International Frankfurt Airport.
(This time we brought our own food!)
Said our tearful goodbyes to my Aunt,
So pleased, the return trip was all good.

Took the plane back to Tampa,
To check on my little Kid's Grandpa.
Then straightaway, getting back in the saddle,
Rode the plane reflectively back home;
Musing nostalgic, heading back to Seattle.

APPRECIATION

My special thanks to my lovely wife, **Lisa**, who has supported me all the way through this long project from the early beginning to the very end.

To my sisters, **Glenda and Lisa**, for their motivational emails and positive feedback and reinforcement.

To **Hans the Mailman**, for imploring me to record my tavern stories and tales for my family and for posterity.

And to **Billy D.**, the die-hard Niners fan, for his sagacious and sophic reviews and inspiring words of advice.

To **Kathy Mierzwa**, my Editor and Book Designer, I give applause and a bow of appreciation. She has brought her professional experience to this enterprise, and inspired me to repair and refine almost every stanza in this book. She has made this venture into a memorable and gratifying undertaking, organizing and actualizing my ramblings into an impressive and illustrious literary work. I am indebted to her commitment to bring this project to fruition, at a much higher level of competence and adept expertise than I could have possibly hoped for. Her skillful proficiency has made for a much more convincing, delightful, and exciting experience for the reader!

BIOGRAPHY

Eric Wolfgang Fotherby was born in 1951
and raised in Allen Park and Warren Michigan;
going from the West side to the East Side
of suburban Detroit.

As a young man he traveled, studied and worked
in Florida, Hawai'i and California
before happily settling in the Northwest,
in the beautiful state of Washington.

He has written stories
of his youthful adventures and travels,
and later-on life experiences,
adding his emotional and gradually-maturing thoughts
as a son, a husband and a father.

He enjoys writing bromantic sports poetry
about his favorite Seattle teams,
in addition to reflections and retrospections
on being an aging, genteel gentleman
who is happily retired
and looking inwardly and outwardly
at a most blessed and appreciated life.

His stories and viewpoints are all in lyric verse
and various rhyme schemes,
using different forms and styles of poetry.

Fotherby feels that a short story
is much more entertaining
if it is lilting and rolling along
in its own rhythms with rhyme,
like a raft on a river or a ship on the sea.

His book is something you can pick up,
put down,
and pick up again later,
for your pleasure,
at your leisure.

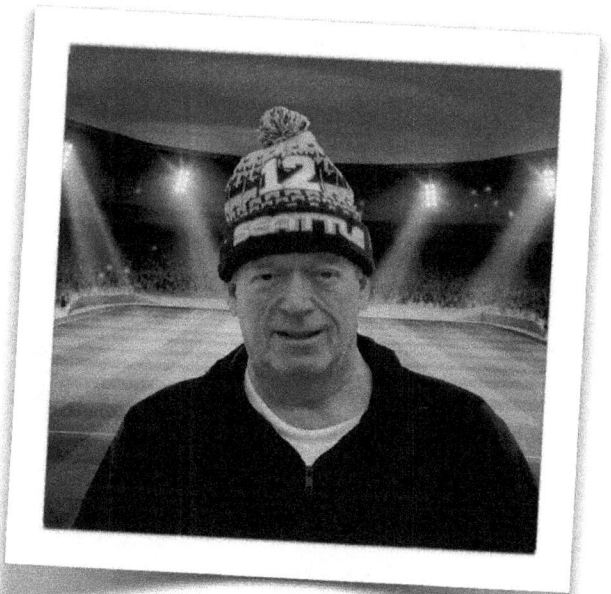

PHOTO CREDITS

Thanks to

Steve Busti / Museum of The Weird in Austin, Texas
For use of the Minnesota Iceman photos, page 13 and 17.

Frontier Fishing Lodge / Northwest Territories, Canada
For use of the the grayling photo page 259.

Paul Richards / The Harvey Richards Media Archive
For use of the Oakland Draft Center image, page 288.

National Transportation Safety Board
For use of the El Faro shipwreck image on page 79.

Murray Lundberg / Yukon Territory Canada
For use of the Alaskan Highway image on page 247.

Nolan Fotherby
For use of the mountain image on page 217.

Hannah Fotherby
For use of the sunset image on page 205.

www.lovebigislandhawaii.com
For use of the Waipi'o Valley image on page 365.

Jackie at Welcome to my Humble Abode on Flickr
For use of the seagull image on page 55. This image has been modified from the original: https://flic.kr/p/hHJSq

Joe Hall on Flickr
For use of the pizza image on page 386. This image has been modified from the original: https://flic.kr/p/adtFeN

INDEX

www.ingramcontent.com/pod-product-compliance
Lightning Source LLC
Chambersburg PA
CBHW071401090426
42737CB00011B/1311